A Good Day in Hell

*The Flatlining of Nurses Across
America
What will it take to Resuscitate our Health
Care System?*

Kellyann Curnayn RN, BSN

xulon
PRESS

A Good Day in Hell
The Flatlining of Nurses Across America
What will it take to Resuscitate our Health Care System?
by Kellyann Curnayn RN, BSN

Printed in the United States of America

ISBN 978-1-60477-172-5

www.xulonpress.com

Acknowledgements

First and foremost I must always thank God who stirred up in me a desire to change the system, the confidence to step out in faith, and humility to know greatness is achieved through serving others. He brought me to a place of humility only to lift me up higher then I could have ever imagined.

My resources were limited to my immediate family and community. My dear husband saw my vision even when I couldn't any longer. Love is a rare gem and my husband is those most precious of them all. My girls have matured into very responsible young ladies and I am so very proud of them. My mother for making me *tough* but with a heart of compassion, these attributes combined allowed me to remain engaged while never helpless (thanks mom, working hard never failed anyone). My girlfriends, I will name them in alphabetical order so as to not pick favorites Cindy, Denise, Donna, Kathy, Katie, MaryLynn and Nikki were all a blessings to me and my children as they often saved them from the boredom of being at home and gave me priceless uninterrupted time to work on the book and my ideas.

Forward

If every Nurse was sent into war, people would be awestruck by what we would accomplish in a crisis. We live the crisis everyday; people continually have needs around us and we feel the pull of triaging on a minute-to-minute basis. The strongest, most knowledgeable, skilled, compassionate, trench digging, crisis-solving bunch of people you could ever want to meet. We beat each other up daily, but would do anything for our wounded comrades when presented with life or death. We are tough; no man or woman alive could get a nurse to do anything she didn't want to unless you implored her heart and then convinced her head. We are warriors, but weary ones, because the battle has been raging for at least twenty years and we are facing increased shortage of troops. So what will it take to turn the odds in our favor? We already know it looks grim from a tactical position. But we have heard many war stories of Lieutenants who accomplished great things with very small armies.

I have been challenged to change the very systems that administration says are immovable; by empowering the voice of those who actually implement the care. Give Nurses a glimmer of hope, by looking at the *real* everyday problems, up close and personal. Fly the battle flag that says we will allow bedside care providers the opportunity to focus on the needs of the patients they first set out to serve. Tell Nurses across the country that relief troops are in the wings. Maybe some of those writing about the war with big initials behind their names (licensed nurses that no longer function at the bedside) could get their hands dirty for awhile until things improve? Have we forgotten the joy of serving? Or has that joy been stolen from us? Charles Stanley taught me this very simple but beautiful truth: "Service is not something you do for God, but something you let God do through you". [1] Will someone enlist in this war, or run to the hills?

Working for a hospital places you right there in the battle. Those doing hand- to-hand combat are the secretaries, patient care assistants and nurses who are given the responsibility to ensure the patients are given the best possible care. Most secretaries and patient care assistants take their responsibilities seriously. But if they don't, the Nurse will single-handedly talk to four different departments, order all the labs, take care of the patient, and then document all the events. The Nurse ends up holding the bag every time. What is the deal with that?

So our moms taught us to pick our battles wisely. James Carville lists the factors he believes go into determining which battles we pick:[2]

a. winnable (our first consideration)
b. important
c. willing to pay the price for winning
d. you're damn sure you can afford to win

Is the battle winnable? Most Nurses have decided it isn't, especially since no one has clearly defined the enemy in this battle. We feel the wind but know not from where it comes. When Nurses are asked what the problems are, at least a hundred little things are mentioned.

Is the battle important? Nationally speaking, yes, but individually, I don't believe any one person has the stamina for this one.

Are we willing to pay the price for winning? Are we prepared for the responsibilities that follow? What form will this victory take? Does it mean more work? Will we have to change? We have checked out long ago, we no longer invest in the outcomes of this unit. We punch in, do our job, and punch out. Our conscience is clear.

Who is our elusive enemy? What makes the job so difficult? When you ask a Nurse what makes her job difficult, the answers vary greatly. Nurses want more money, which is understandable, but the salary they receive is not the cause of the job dissatisfaction. It seems no one can clearly define the "why" behind the shortage of Nurses.

How defeating to see a problem that has no viable solution. This is the first and greatest reason as to why the Nursing shortage will soon become a national crisis. Who will fight the powers that be to allow people to begin serving again? Something crushes the spirits and bodies of bedside care providers everyday while others elude the trampling.

Table of Contents

Chapter One
What has happened to the *esteemed* Profession
of Nursing?..13

Chapter Two
The Heart of a Servant 21

Chapter Three
The Heart of an Institution 41

Chapter Four
Inner City Nursing 49

Chapter Five
Merks Manual of Nursing Shortage.................59

Chapter Six
War Room 85
Inside Look into a Nursing Unit 85

Chapter Seven
    Nursing *Units*..95
    Shouldn't that mean teamwork? 95

Chapter Eight
    Mother Theresa CEO 113

Chapter Nine
    The Path from Me to We................................131

Chapter 1

What Happened to the *esteemed* Profession of Nursing?

When I began my career in 1991 I would take care of six very ill patients and go home with the great feeling of job well done. I knew their names, I was genuinely concerned about their immediate needs, and I proactively looked to their future needs. My peers were also concerned with the well being of all the patients. What has changed? Every person I know who has been a Nurse of more then fifteen years can tell you something has changed and no one can pinpoint what has happened. So now I go into work, I'm assigned four relatively well patients and I can barely get my work done. I go home frustrated and angry wondering why I couldn't give the care I wanted to. I barely have time to learn their names and being proactive about future needs is the last thing on my triage list, which doesn't bode well for the patient.

Ann Lander wrote an article on October 11, 1998

Fort Wayne, Ind.: I was an RN, and so was my mother before me. I've advised my two daughters to go to business school and forget about nursing. The work is brutal, and there's no satisfaction anymore—- only guilt because you can't do a decent job. It's a mess. Ann

In this article Ann Landers prints the opinion of 10 Nurses from across the U.S. and ends the article with this.

I had hoped to balance this column by printing some letters from nurses who were happy in their profession, but there weren't any. How sad. Unless something is done to help our nurses, there won't be any, and we will be up that well-known creek without a paddle.[3]

When the activities of the day result in less than optimal care the end result is intangible frustration on the part of health care workers. It is a combination of feeling guilty and yet victimized which then results in dissonance within the person. The Nurse does not know where the source of blame should be placed. Hence the blame is displaced randomly as situations present themselves. The resonating sound heard from administration is an incoherent murmuring of complaints that don't seem to add up to anything.

What has been done to improve the work conditions of Nurses? Well now in 2007 we are experiencing an increased shortage of *warm bodies* and those left on the frontline have become weary, disgusted, and disillusioned which sometimes can be seen as having a bad attitude. Lets do some long term studies and questionnaires of those entering the field and then revisit them one, two, and thee years later. People don't want to hear the truth.

The attributes of a person who has chosen Nursing as a profession are what most would consider honorable. Nurses are among the most highly trusted profession even above doctors. Honorable doesn't change a system gone bad, honorable doesn't pay the bills and yet this book is written to seek out the honorable. The system has stolen the joy of serving and the system has turned a deaf ear to the flesh and bones of the institution.

Who says "NO" to governing bodies, who says this policy does not increase the safety or quality of care we give our patients. That's right, no one does. Because any time a hospital must experience the assault of an unexpected visit from an accrediting agency, they burn and itch like a bad case of herpes until they get rid of them. The instructions are do whatever they tell you, say yes maam, yes sir, and get rid of them as quickly as possible. Which, if they want to get funded for their Medicare patients, they better do just that. Who are they accountable to? They have become the antithesis to themselves.

Who tells these governing bodies their mandates are not feasible to implement outside the bubble they live in? Everyone in a hospital can make rules, but when the day is done, the Nurse and those who work directly with the Nurse are left holding the bag. This elusive bag is weighing us down and drowning the profession. The contents are the hundred little things that make the day "more difficult." No one item creates the weight, but combined, it is the root cause of the Nursing shortage—or, at the very least, the dissatisfaction of those currently in the profession.

Hospitals need to get back to the basics; whom do we all serve? The patient of course and the harsh reality is the system sets us up for failure. By making it clear, document the care, mark off the check list and use our money saving dispensing machines and after you do all that, if there is time, yes you can also take care of the patient. The system was etherized into the above state of affairs and the bedside care givers and patients are the ones experiencing the distress induced under the guise of patient safety standards. They have made the trivial important and the important trivial and now nobody knows what or whom they are suppose to be serving anymore.

What happens when those who actually implement the care tell those in management we can't implement the policy the way it is written? The general rule is sorry someone even more powerful then myself stated it must be implemented that way.

The *Chicken Soup for the Soul* series includes a book written specifically about Nurses and the wonderful stories they have to tell about how they made a difference in the lives of others. This book is not intended to be the Anti-*Chicken Soup for the Soul*, but to serve as more of a reality check to the problems that exist within the inpatient world. Nurses continually rise above job dissatisfaction and give wonderful care, but the profession is burdened. No one wants to moan and groan about a problem they can't fix. The Nursing shortage rages and the solutions proposed today are the same ones proposed twenty years ago. The only difference is now the country has a stake in what is quickly becoming a national crisis. Nursing is a huge stake in the financing of American health care.

When dealing with a problem, it is difficult to sound positive, and yet we want our Nurses in America to give the profession a better image by talking more positively about Nursing. Who will stand up for the Nurse? To date, everyone wants us to feel appreciated while we work within a system that does not allow us to do the very job we were hired to do. For those in administration, put on a pair of scrubs and spend a day with your frontline; you would have a greater understanding.

Any part of the system that doesn't improve the quality or safety of care we give our patients should be eliminated. We have paperwork, checklists, and charting systems all mandated by someone with the patient's best interest in mind, supposedly. And yes, in theory, so many of those things "seem" to improve patient safety standards. But in actuality, they remove the Nurse from the bedside, and when that happens, all standards are lowered. This has been proven. So we have people with lots of fancy titles coming up with lots of amazing ways to improve the quality of care we give our patients, but no one hears the Nurse: "We can not effectively work under the current work settings that are being placed before us."

Who suffers for all the checks and balances? Ultimately, the patient, the very person we are trying to protect. As well as the weary Nurse who struggles each and every day with whom to serve first, the system or the patient. Yes, I say "we," because I am a Nurse. No fancy titles or job description, I work as a bedside care provider living the day in and day out frustrations. So hold on tightly, because this book is going to be a wild ride. Unedited, or, more importantly, not politically correct, view point of the problems that exist within the world of inpatient care.

I don't know about those reading this, but I do not recommend my children take on Nursing as a profession. How sad is this, because one of my daughters truly has the heart of a servant.

There will be times when it sounds as though I'm portraying Nursing in a bad light. Nurses have developed coping mechanisms that are not healthy. Those behaviors have turned into some very unhealthy/ toxic environments, which are contributing to the "bad press" that our collegiate elite refer to. I will describe this environment in detail while maintaining my stand that that the chicken (difficult environment) came before the egg (dysfunctional behavior). All institutions should start promoting their frontline, not everyone promoting upper administration. I suggest that no one understands the heart, mind and frustrations of a Nurse except the Nurse on the front line.

I have a theory on Nursing called Labor Pains of Nursing. Who recalls the pain of birth? The woman laboring and only she. No one else around her can feel the pain at that moment of birth. The truth is, we forget the intensity of it, and any Nurse who has left the bedside has forgotten the intensity of the daily frustrations that make the job so difficult.

So we have administration looking to nurse managers, who are Nurses, after all. We as Nurses don't fit any business model out there, and our dysfunctional family is impenetrable to anyone wearing a suit. We demand respect, and it takes a lot of hard work to gain our respect. Our standards are higher than anyone could mandate; we just need to be allowed to start loving again the job we set out to do.

Business Scenario

Imagine for weeks and months you walked into your job with the intention of serving your boss (for us, patients) with the best of your abilities, but every day your efforts were thwarted by a system that wouldn't allow you to do that. You arrive at 8:30 because of your eagerness to start the day right, but at 9:20, you're still getting briefed on the boss' agenda. You begin by getting copies for a presentation she has at 10:00. The person who was supposed to make copies is at break or not in sight. No problem, you think to yourself, I can make copies. So you wait in line (place your orders on the rack). From a distance, you hear your boss. At 9:55, your boss wants to know where his presentation is. 10:05, the boss is not happy, because he is late and it was entirely your fault.

We move on to the next task. By the way, the employee in charge of copies is still no where to be found. Your boss arrives back at 12:30. You were about to go to lunch; your boss had lunch during the presentation. The new proposal (drug) is to arrive from Pharmland and he wanted to review it on a full stomach. You try to tell him it really doesn't matter if he reviews it (takes his meds) on an empty stomach, but that just won't do. So at 12:30 you call Pharmland to see where the proposal is. Their staff indicates it is not an emergency and they are prioritizing. You receive the proposal at 14:00, and once again, your boss (patient) is not happy with you. Basically, you border on incompetence as far as she is concerned.

How long would you hold the standard until you decided your conscience was clear and give up? Can anyone afford to care about a problem they cannot fix themselves and see no possible resolution to be had from management? It is just too emotionally draining. The aftermath is a punch in, punch out mentality. We survive knowing we work only three or four days a week, and we punch out feeling it is no longer our problem.

Chapter Two

The Heart of a Servant

We are never really happy until we experience the joy of serving others.

S o if the above statement is true, I had better give some practical advice on how to obtain a state of happiness. We all have people and places that we have been given the responsibility to serve. Having someone else's benefit as our main concern is a good indication that we are in fact serving.

Attributes of a servant

1. kind
2. loving
3. gentle
4. selfless

Can't say I'm the epitome of kind, loving, gentle and selfless. So I don't resemble the attributes of a servant, but yet I tell you all, that is the path to personal fulfillment. Ahh, I left out that you must let Christ serve through you, and when you allow that to happen, you have moments that resemble those four attributes. Charles Stanley states, "True service is not something we do for God, but rather something God does through us".[4] So the kicker here is, you don't have to be Mother Theresa to begin serving.

Recall for a moment something you did that was genuinely selfless and kind. Take a moment and reflect.

It feels good; it is an unadulterated good feeling. You didn't buy it, smoke it, drink it, or inject it, and yet somehow you felt just great. Why don't we turn toward that free high God gives? Who would have thought good old fashioned service could make you feel so good? The spiritual highs in life are experienced through Christ-like service. Satan's tool of deception is that you must serve yourself first to get that high.

Have you ever wondered how that Italian mom just cooked day after day, for parties, communions, weddings, every living day of her life? I personally have. The stereotypical Italian mom served her family and got joy and fulfillment from that service. To take her out of the kitchen would have stolen her joy and brought on her eventual death. I personally hate to cook and my husband loves good food. So I try to make fancy meals occasionally and guess what? It brings me joy. His joy is my joy, and it all started out with me doing an act of kindness that I hate doing. You must serve in some capacity or you will have difficulty appreciating and seeing those that serve you each and every day.

Do you think every restaurant meal was prepared by a person with the heart of a servant? We would like to think so, but how many chefs feel unappreciated for the work they do? The chef no longer is a faceless entity but a man filled with vim and vigor making the meal I ordered.

When my aunt was in the hospital, I asked her if she would give me the honor of giving her a bath. She didn't want me to serve her in that fashion, but at the same time she wanted to be bathed. Water is the symbol of renewal and strength. I challenge all my readers to not bathe or brush your teeth for three days. (Don't really do this. If I sell a millions of copies we could have some serious environmental issues). You would feel just nasty by the third day. When hospital staff become overburdened with tasks, people so often place a tub of water in front of the patient (if they're lucky) and say bathe yourself. Yes, their arms work, but they still are in the hospital, which would lead me to believe *they are sick*. Imagine you had the flu and someone placed a basin of water in front of you. Well, that is how a sick patient in the hospital feels. When the health care provider picks up the wash cloth and assists with the back and then begins to let the warm clean water pour over the head and neck, the patient become renewed and strengthened, and I personally become spiritually renewed through the service I provide. My job makes me bigger than

I am. It allows me the opportunity to feel the joy of serving. And get this one. I get paid to do it. Cha-ching! Don't tell me God isn't good.

What does it mean to be a servant? Well, I can tell you what God had to say about being a servant. The Lord Jesus Christ came to serve (Mark 10:45) and He sees all believers as servants in His Father's kingdom. (John 20:21). First Thessalonians 5:24 says: The one who calls you is faithful and he will do it. This simply means that God assumes full responsibility for enabling us to carry out the work He assigns.

Work He assigns in the life and day of a nurse. Never ending work. We start the day with an assigned number of patients. Review orders, history, and medications, receive report and start the day out running. The part that kills me is no one has scheduled into my day the unexpected MI or the horrible diarrhea. Oh yes, it has all happened to me personally. So the latter of the two can wait while I give my morning medications. Is that really fair? Who will help serve the patient? Who takes into account his day? And isn't that the bigger question?

Does the charge nurse care or is she too over-burdened? Does the secretary care? Maybe she will help me out a little more. You know, with stuff I'm supposed to do. Or is she too overburdened? Does the patient care assistant care, or is she to overbur-dened also?. We can't do it alone because the way I see it, no one is really happy anywhere. They have learned to work the system so they feel as little pain as possible. Do nurses support each other consistently? Nurses feel so burnt out they can't even think of supporting each other. Will they serve their fellow nurses or are they done serving after feeling duped by a system that is structured with the unwritten rule every man for himself?

Is it just a job? I guess there are those who think of it that way. But come on, guys. We are hired to serve people, and let's say in a million and one ways. The most demanding places to work are on the units where the nurses have four or more patients. The demands are impossible to keep up with, assuming you have remained faithful to the cause and the welfare of your patients is your greatest concern. I read a great phrase once: If you have to choose between pleasing God or pleasing man, choose God. He is more likely to remember. When we make paperwork our first priority, we choose man to please. I'm writing this book and created this business because I know first-hand how hard it is to tend to my patients first. As for me and my house, we will serve the Lord. I began asking myself, does anyone really care? I worked for an institution where the top really did care but didn't know how to get the changes implemented in the trenches. Which again is why I began this effort. I had to quit or stay on the pot. (just for the record I'm still on the pot)

Charles Stanley wrote

> "Ministry occurs when the divine resources of God meet a human need through a loving servant."[5]

Ministry occurs daily in the lives of every hospital employee whether they realize it or not. We impact the lives of so many. A Nurse working full time on a med surg floor will interact with at least twelve patients and their family members in a week's time. Twelve people who are experiencing a life crisis and their family members (and we know everyone has the most functional families even in good times). Talk about ministry! We are given the responsibility to administer care but also to foresee future and immediate needs through our expert medical knowledge.

All employees are contractually hired to serve in some capacity. But here we are talking about hospital employees who should keep in the forefront of their mind there are patients at the end of this service line. Unless you have ever been a patient in a hospital, you can't really understand the vulnerability of that role. I was so humbled when I had to put on the gown (without a bra), or at least my breasts were humbled. I have assisted hundreds of patients in the process of getting a chest x-ray, but yet I had no idea what if felt like until placed in that circumstance.

Trust in God and leave all the consequences to him. So I'm saying depend on God to help you through the day. Yes, that is exactly right. When I choose to serve my patients first, God often gives the time back to me. There is a twist to trusting in God. If you want his peace, you also will have to listen to the answers he provides. Our God is not a helpless God. He knows readily what needs to happen to change the situation. Are you ready to step out in faith? Try it. Step out in faith, place your patients first. The day ends and I'm thinking "you're just amazing, God." Because I made the better choice of serving my patients, he gave the time back to me. The feeling of a job well done gets me past the dissatisfaction on those days that I do end up staying late. The bottom line is;

The system must change and our hearts must also change

Which leads us to this book.

When do we need the consoler, the peace that only God can give? Well, let me tell you, sisters and brothers, I need it every waking minute, but when I'm at work I'm asking for the Holy Spirit to make his presence known on a second by second basis. My attitude can change in a heartbeat. So get your attitude right with what is important and start changing the rest.

What is your attitude?

1. Another miserable day on this lousy floor
2. I think I can, I think I can
3. Maybe today won't be so crazy and I can actually sit down to eat for a whole thirty minutes
4. Oh lord, I'm just not ready for the preceptor whose whole intent is to make me feel as humanly stupid as possible.
5. Just get through it, just do what needs to be done, speak only when spoken to.

(Did you realize if you looked pissed off all the time the patients don't even want to speak with you).

6. I will take care of my patients and my patients alone; I cannot be concerned with anything else occurring on the floor. It is just not my problem.

7. Today is going to be a good day. I will provide excellent care and be a support to my fellow team members.

So we have a profession of people who can directly relate to the above statements and yet no one addresses the environment.

Yes, I want to have a Christ-like attitude but martyrdom is not my strong point. I could serve faithfully and remain frustrated or dissect the problem with some passion.

One day I received a patient that had been deemed *difficult* by the staff, and rightfully so. I was not at all pleased with being assigned to this person. But what happened was just a miracle, I said in the quiet of my heart, "Well, Lord, you sent us here to be servants". In a moment my whole attitude changed. I don't even recall the rest of the night. When the attitude of my heart was changed, it was no longer an obstacle but a blessing. Once my thought process was in line with Christ, he sent the consoler. This event occurred over ten years ago and it still speaks to my heart today.

What areas of my own life do I not serve Christ with a servant's heart?

When I placed this statement in the forefront, it encompassed far more reaching areas than just my career. As a woman, did I serve my own family with the level of service I was looking for in hospital employees? I should give even better service to my family than I do to my patients, shouldn't I? Could I wake up each morning, make breakfast, clean the kitchen, do laundry and pick up around the house day after day and feel content and peaceful that my service is onto the Lord (which means I couldn't complain)? Ouch, did that hurt. God has a way of exposing our own sin when we think we're trying to help another. I didn't get enough recognition for my menial tasks of maintaining a house and I didn't find joy in doing it. Now this is where the heart of service gets it first workout. I was blessed beyond measure with healthy children, a great husband and a full pantry of food. So maybe God could take away my blessings to help me see the bigger picture; I would have no messes to clean up after, no house to clean, and no husband to pick up after, and I could stop down at the homeless shelter for a hot meal. So I began soul-searching and slowly my heart changed.

So when Christ makes his presence known and gives us his direction for service, do we shrink because we thought God would give us a loftier calling? I'm much too important to hand out newspapers, help clean the church or help out with the kids. When I was getting trained as an ICU Nurse I became indignant to the caliber of patients they gave me (it makes my heart shudder just to write about it). I knew I was a great Nurse, practitioner and nurturer, but yet I was not getting challenging ICU patients. I received every chronic John Doe (alcoholic) and cancer patient (family or patient in denial about the obvious outcome). I didn't like my job for the reasons described in the previous chapter (increased tasks and decreased time to actually care for the patient), but now this was just insult to injury.

One day I finally got it. I confessed to God I would lovingly serve the destitute and dying and do it with Christ-like service. Within a week, he released me from that job and unit that I disliked so much. What areas of your life are you resisting to serve Christ? He loves you too much to stop badgering you. Surrender to his will. Trust me, it is the least painful choice, but even more importantly, it's where the greatest blessings await.

Allowing God to lead seems scary and is often associated with hard work, but can anyone love us more then God does? These passages, reference a loving father and they have always given me an insight into his goodness and compassion.

Matthew 7: 9-12

> Which of you, if his son asks for bread, will give him a stone? Or if he asks for a fish, will give him a snake? If you, then, though you are evil, know how to give good gifts to your children, how much more will your Father in heaven give good gifts to those who ask

him! So in everything, do to others what you
would have them do to you, for this sums up
the Law and the Prophets.

Jesus Christ himself came to serve, so who on
earth feels they are above Jesus in action or spirit?
Even if you don't practice Christianity, there is
nothing in the biography of Jesus that would indicate anything but an upright, hard-working man who
had some awesome gifts. Did he abuse his authority
over others? Did he take the cake walk job while his
subordinates washed the feet of his guests?

To serve is to be likened to something we are not
naturally inclined to do or our spirits must be coaxed
to believe it is the right thing to do. I believe if inpatient hospital staff were held accountable to each
other for the service they provide they would learn
the joy of serving. Someone once told me you cannot
mandate or enforce team work and service. Truly I
say to all, how does the person hanging around the
corner doing the bare minimum to make the day pass
feel at the end of a day? Do they go home with a clear
conscience of a job well done? Maybe by encouraging, mandating and enforcing such behavior,
people will experience the joy of serving. When it is
all said and done we don't really have a choice; there
are patients on the other end of this service line.

Oswald Chambers quoted it perfectly:

"If our devotion is to the cause of humanity,
we will be quickly defeated and broken-

hearted, since we will often be confronted with a great deal of ingratitude from other people. But if we are motivated by our love for God, no amount of ingratitude will be able to hinder us from serving one another".[6]

A Nurses spirituality is nourished each and every time she performs a task with a genuine desire to serve without regard to the worthiness of the recipient or the potential of the reward. Nurses are brilliant, and yet have to perform tasks that would be considered the lowest of the low. The task does not define who we are, and in actuality makes us so much bigger, we increase our capacity to care each and every time we serve another. I have grown spiritually and professionally primarily because the circumstances made me grow, not because I was so mature that I looked for opposition and trials to help me become a better person. God is the most awesome Father, He has a way of making us functional. The more you get challenged, the stronger you become.

Milton Katselas writes in his book *Dreams into Action.*

"What you do is not as vital as how you do it. The how is taking hold of your job and your life in an exciting, active, and caring way".[7]

Empowered people motivated with genuine desire to serve others cannot help but get blessed while blessing others. It is just truly amazing. These are some of the miracles I want to see, people transforming their lives from one of self-centeredness to one of service. No human being knows the spirit of a man except the man himself, anymore than anyone knows the mind and ways of God other than the Holy Spirit of God.

What is our genuine human nature apart from the grace of God? Human nature left to itself searches always to first satisfy ego versus altruism, take versus give, finding fault versus finding good. What wellspring do you tap into to regain the healing powers of renewal to go into work afresh each day? The reality is we have Catholic, Baptist, Methodist and Seven Day Adventist hospitals (to name a few), but to date I have never seen an "Atheist Hospital." People of America have founded this country on the common belief that in God we Trust. If we could all go back to that place of trust.

What makes us not see the truth in any given situation? The Bible says our own unrighteousness clouds the truth from our very eyes. To realize how I need to improve means I may need to change and I don't have energy for that either. The Old Testament tells of how the Israelites begged to go back to Egypt into slavery. It was all they knew, and that which we know is more comforting than the unknown, even if it does present itself in the form of slavery.

Are Nurse enslaved? And if so, to whom? We are slaves to the phone, checklists, policies, people, and computers. The chains were placed on the profession with such incremental steps no one really can define the exactness of the problem. Old Scrooge can hear the chains rattling for miles and the ghosts of Nurses will be all that is left as we try to staff inpatient hospital units.

The profession is oppressed by policies, checklists and tasks. So when left in a state of helplessness, we become paralyzed or strike out.

Moses lived a privileged life in the courts of Pharaoh. He didn't experience the hardship that his brethren did. He was not considered slave or bondservant. But when the truth of what was occurring rang true to his heart, he struck out. He saw an Egyptian abusing his brethren and struck him to the ground, killing him, and hid him in the sand. The scriptures don't lead us to believe he had taken action before this point. Helplessness causes us to strike out; usually striking out doesn't help but hinders. Nurses are striking out at each other every day. He allowed himself to see and feel the distress of his people, he acted out and ran away. He ran into the desert to the land of Gideon. He took a wife, had children and removed himself from the distress he felt. Registered Nurses are running away from the inpatient setting and removing themselves from the distress of working at the bedside. Although he realized the injustice of what was occurring, he ran away.

Helplessness is quite paralyzing. Taking action is empowering. Communist parties rule through helplessness; your lives will be miserable unless you do exactly what this government tells you to do. No one individual could stand up to a government; which is why America stands up against communism. Who stands up for the Nurse? Who goes to battle to defend our licenses? Nurses functioning at the bedside are paralyzed in a state of inaction. Alone we are so very vulnerable, but when backed up by an authority above us we are empowered. Physicians have the AMA, which is a very powerful organization. Who with actual power stands behind the Nurse? To date, everyone appeases either their own bosses or ultimately governing bodies that hand down jurisdictions. When Moses met God at the mountain top and experienced God at the place where the flames did not consume the bush, he was empowered. If we are on God's mission, the flames will not consume us any more than they did that bush, but there will be times it will get pretty hot and you will feel like you are getting consumed. God will not keep us from the flames but he has promised to meet us in the middle of that fiery inferno. But if God is for us, who can be against us? God has seen the injustices that have been done to the profession and heard your cries. We can go out not with our own authority but with the knowledge that God goes before us.

Dr. Pastor Joel Hunter illustrated this point during a sermon.

Certain authority you have when you are on God's mission. Remember when you were in school and the teacher would have a special assignment for you to do during class? The only reason she asked you is because she deemed you worthy, and can you recall the feeling of importance? You got a letter or hall pass from the teacher; she trusted you enough to give you this "special" assignment. Did you hold that piece of paper and think, "Yeah, stop me. I dare you. I have a letter from my teacher to be in these halls." The thing that gave you power was her authority, not your authority. When you are on a mission from God, it is his authority you function under.

> "The reasonable man adapts himself to the world; the unreasonable one persists in trying to adapt the world to himself. Therefore, all progress depends on the unreasonable man."[8]
>
> ~George Bernard Shaw

Nurses have been quite reasonable for a long time; we have adapted ourselves through the inundation of phones, computers, and legalities. The profession has maintained a continued murmuring of dissatisfaction for over twenty years and now it is time the litigiousness of providing care come to odds with the reality of what it takes to provide that care. Your policies, checklists and tasks are hurting the very people you say you want to protect and serve. But look, dear patients of America, we who hold all the power, ensure your safety from our ivory towers, while the bondservants are instructed on proper implementation.

It is easy to have a bias against a group of people until you get to know them. When someone becomes emotionally attached it is then more difficult to oppress them. Moses became emotionally attached and could no longer watch his people experience oppression.. Which is why I suggest over and over again throughout this book, put on a pair of scrubs and spend a day with a Nurse. When a bedside Nurse gets out of working at the bedside, she will say, "Whew! Am I glad I don't have to do that anymore."

Luke 16:13

> "No servant can serve two masters. Either he will hate the one and love the other, or he will be devoted to the one and despise the other."

The two masters we as Nurses serve are the "elusive bag" weighing us down and the patient. The scripture above says we will be devoted to the one and despise the other. We buck the system or just check out, and our unwillingness to get involved in any given institution speaks for itself. We dislike the system and have remained faithful to our object of service. We have chosen the better master, and the fact that we continue to remain unhappy speaks for itself. Administration remains baffled as to why they can't get the buy in from Nurses. The system has made it clear: hospitals serve many entities, ranging from governing bodies, policy makers, HMO's, stock holders, and insurance companies. The Nurse knows that it doesn't matter how much that new process burdens her and doesn't improve the care she gives, she will be shackled with the responsibility of carrying it out. Administration wants to know why they can't get buy-in from Nurses. We have not completely surrendered to apathy, and if we had, the silence would be deafening.

So a true servant cannot serve themselves and the patient. In the course of the day did any Nurse say let's see how my needs could be met today? That is not at all what happened, but something did go astray. Do I love the object of my service? Well, maybe we can't always use the word love, but we do genuinely care. I must always think of what is in the best interest of my patients, spiritually, emotionally and physically. We as health care professionals are legally required to ensure excellent health care is given. We as health care professionals administer that care in an efficient manner. But it goes beyond that. We genuinely care, and yes, sometimes we try to stretch ourselves to Christ-like service and love.

Matthew 9:5

> Which is easier to say, 'your sins are forgiven' or to say, 'Get up and walk'?

My question to all hospitals across America is:

Which is easier to say, 'we create safe policies' or to say, 'we give excellent care'?

Which is easier to say, 'we care', or to say, 'I will care for you'?

Action will always speak louder then words and action is what is needed to change this situation.

Matthew 6:1-2

"Be careful not to do your 'acts of righteousness' before men, to be seen by them. If you do, you will have **no** reward from your Father in heaven.

So when you give to the needy, do not announce it with trumpets, as the hypocrites do in the synagogues and on the streets to be honored by men. I tell you the truth they have received their reward **in full**."

If you get your reward from men, by publicly announcing your greatness and awesome deeds, thus taking down the team, Jesus says you have received your reward **in full.** Well, you got your reward and God always means what he says. Jesus said *in full* and that is just what he meant. Don't expect Peter to pat you on the back for a job well done while you're passing the pearly gates. We have been uniquely designed and chosen to serve a Father who sees what is done in secret, and God himself will reward us. Let's reflect whose reward will be better, God's or the accolades of men. Earthly reward vs. eternal reward. Hmmm.I suggest you not think on that one for too long.

Chapter Three

The Heart of an Institution

You can't physically and or mentally survive with a real and true picture of all the needs a nursing unit presents in the course of the day. I believe hospital staff have been dulled and are not even conscious of what has occurred. We need a rekindling of the spirit, a reawakening to the call of service, but this does not apply to just nurses; I'm talking about all inpatient hospital staff. The Nursing shortage is a matter of the heart, but the heart does not just pump at the bedside. Each department either continues to help that heart pump or contributes to congestive heart failure (overburdened work force, fatigue), hardening of the arteries (apathy), myocardial infarction (Nurse gone Postal), and then general myopathy (there is no oomph left to pump anything worth while, just the constant ebb and flow of blood into the right side and out the left.) The body knows it's not getting enough oxygenated blood with each beat, but it can't do a thing about it. The symptoms just keep getting worse.

So everyone agrees that the heart of an institution doesn't pump at the bedside. But are we training, orienting and reminding ALL hospital employees about whom they serve and how their job directly affects the outcomes of our patients (product, customers, front line). Even if the institution does present an altruistic approach with its initial orientation, we must have a system in place that reorients and holds accountable all staff to this very fact.

Ultimate accountability is placed on the Nurse, the whole system could fail but she is held responsible for the care of the patient. The medication took three hours to come up from pharmacy, yeh,yeh we don't want to hear it. The lab values took four hours to post results, yeh, yeh, we don't want to hear it. Environmental hasn't cleaned the room so I can't take that patient, yeh yeh, well you get the point. No one wants to hear it, so who does a Nurse turn to when thing go awry.

This is the dilemma I'm in; I keep talking to Nurses who verbalize the same complaints. Discussing problems is viewed as not being positive. She is just a little too impassioned, "a wild card." Impassioned about what? Quality patient care. We could think of solutions on our own time or we could punch out and leave the problems behind. I've personally done both. During the process of writing this book, I have wavered between wanting to punch out and wanting to discuss the problems. We are exhausted at the end of the day. We go home and vent to our loved ones; they patiently listen.

I can't speak for the rest of America, but my husband was sick of listening (to the problems). He is now an avid listener to my possible resolutions. If you don't like your job, quit, because I'm sick of listening to it. I asked a well-respected and awarded Nurse, "What could we do to make our jobs better/ easier?" The answer was, "The only thing that makes this job easier is if you don't give a shit."

This Nurse did give excellent care and did "give a shit," but despite the personal high work ethic, that Nurse couldn't come up with a more viable solution. The Nurse went on to say that there was no changing the system, so just live with it. So **not** caring makes the job easier, and I believe in the course of a day you must continually choose what you will care about.

I worked with another Nurse who stated she loved her job. Which she did — it was evident in her work and her attitude. Her full time job was as an educator at the local college, and she was making some extra money over the summer break. I affirmed her excellent work ethic and pointed out that even though she took excellent care of her patients she did not invest in the needs of the floor and, for that matter, the needs of all the patients. She agreed whole heartedly without hesitation.

To begin the heart-to-heart conversations my first question would be. What is the difference between a human being under your care vs. a human being under someone else's care? People (everyone who passes through nursing units) will see and hear the needs that present on an inpatient floor but can ignore the call light of a patient or the request of a family member because that patient is not "theirs." Thus human beings have been given levels of importance based on who is legally required to render the services.

My dissatisfaction comes from constantly having to fight a system that will not allow me to do the job that I love so much, combined with constantly being aware of the multitude of needs around me. I went on to ask above Nurse if she could do this job on a full-time basis. The answer was a definitive NO. That is where the answer lies—there is a Pandora's Box that someone doesn't want opened. Until we find out the contents of the above Nurse's "NO," the dissatisfaction of Nurses across America will continue.

> "You'd have to be crazy to take a horse over a jump without having checked to see what's on the other side of it first. But for some reason it's considered acceptable to take blind leaps in business."[9]

Has anyone considered if the horse is in the middle of a blazing inferno? Rumor has it, there is a nursing shortage and the alchemists don't predict the heavens to open up and send more any time soon. The shortage is soon to be national crisis and we had better make that horse jump. The above quote caught my attention not because the author is necessarily wrong, but this is not the approach to take when presented with such a dilemma. Hospitals wouldn't call what they do everyday business; we have physically ill patients looking for care. It would appear administration does consider it everyday business since they continue to add job complexity to our jobs. Let's start asking the nurses the heart-to-heart questions, without administrative influences lacing the conversation. If you get a nurse talking about what makes the job so difficult, she could give you story after story. He or she could talk for hours (I've done a lot of listening). Administration can't handle the truth (picture Jack Nicholson as he screams the statement at Tom Cruise), and if they allowed themselves to hear the truth they wouldn't know what to do with it. Ignoring the problems hasn't helped. Best throw caution to the wind, guys, and start coming up with some innovative ideas. As I'm sure you all suspect, I think I have a few of those ideas, but of course you will have to read on.

Those who have managed to deflect the stresses of everyday life of inpatient care have been deafened to the clamor of teamwork. And why, because that means they may have to jump back into the fiery inferno and for what? For the good of all or the good of every patient that walks through those doors. "I'm going to get burned and you're not going to change a thing." I'll be left with a new imposed system of nursing and I'm going to have to find a new avenue to escape the pressures of everyday. The current hell I live with is better then the hell I don't know about. To quote Shakespeare,

To grunt and sweat under a weary life,
But that the dread of something after
　　death,—
The undiscover'd country, from whose
　　bourn
No traveller returns,—puzzles the will,
And makes us rather bear those ills we have
Than fly to others that we know not of?

Nurses are done, they want out, and if they can't get out, they find the work around. The "work around" presents itself in many forms, preceptor, charge nurse, assignment espionage, or tunnel vision.

Everyone of our clients/customer/revenue producing people are sick (not that corporate America doesn't have its fair share of not well people, but we're not obligated to have compassion for their illnesses). So every employee within a hospital should do their job, knowing it is the patients they serve. Well, that's a tall order to fill, so I'm starting with the appetizer (this book).

Careful business theory is being applied to front line workers of hospital staff. It was also applied to health care years ago, and we all know where the state of health care is right now. You don't think this affects you. Let's reflect on the gasoline shortage of 1979, lines of people waiting days to get a tank of gas. Close your eyes and picture people waiting to get health care. How will the nation determine who gets the available beds?

In April 2006, officials with the Health Resources and Services Administration (HRSA) released projections that the nation's nursing shortage would grow to more than one million nurses by the year 2020. In the report titled *What is Behind HRSA's Projected Supply,Demand, and Shortage of Registered Nurses?*, analysts show that all 50 states will experience a shortage of nurses to varying degrees by the year 2015.[10]

The whole hospital must be ready to serve at any minute. People are your product; human lives with a crisis. When the alarm goes off at 5:00 a.m., my response is "work keeps you honest." The reality is, my work makes me bigger than I am; it raises me far above the level of honesty. I contractually agree to serve the patients within an institution for an hourly salary. Everyday I go to work, I receive the blessing of being more than I really am, serving others even if I don't feel like doing it. I'm not sure Corporate America compares to the inner strength and talent of hospital employees. We have to do our jobs knowing it is the patient we serve, not some potential customer who will buy the product. Our product is our customer, and we can't come up with marketing schemes to get more money out of them. We have to first serve them to the best of our ability, and then administration is stuck with the daunting task of trying to ensure they get paid for those services.

I would love to see a corporation give their product or services away on a regular basis with the hope of getting paid for at least the cost of production. I am disillusioned by bureaucracies and their functioning, but I still have compassion and empathy for hospitals who are trying to fight the entanglement of a health care system gone bad. Hospitals today have to barter and beg to get paid for the services rendered. Fortunately this is not the battle I have been inspired to fight, but it is surely one that needs a good leader.

With all due respect to the business world, we are dealing with people's lives, not products at the end of an assembly line. We need to take the business models that hospitals are using and rethink the whole thing. One institution I worked for did just that—they rearranged the model to focus on the care of the patient and how the staff did that. The model looked and sounded great but will it ever get implemented? Those who come up with the models should be required to help implement t them on the floors (in a pair of scrubs of course). Every institution should review the *model* they have archived in some book and take an honest reflection, is the printed actually implemented?

Chapter Four

Inner City Nursing

Let's reflect on the inner city kid who has suffered at the hand of abuse. He grows up in a tough neighborhood and hence grows up quite tough. Nurses work in a tough neighborhood and hence grow up quite tough. Schools have seen children slip into a state of continued trouble that eventually leads to incarceration in correctional institutes. Institutions have seen Nurses slip into a state of apathy, and the profession is experiencing a national shortage. When someone tries to reach the heart of a troubled child, what happens? Unless the adult has the firm intent to persevere, the inner city child will remain ungrateful and abusive. They give Nurses gift certificates and praise, and then we slip back into our own way of functioning. In the child's mind, you're just another miserable adult who will let them down. In the mind of the Nurse you're not going to change one thing that makes this job difficult, so what, again, do you want out of me? How do you gain that child's trust?

You don't give up, you continue to say with *actions,* "I do care." Eventually the barriers come down and the child learns to trust again.

What has anyone done, through *actions, to* prove to the Nurse that they really want to change things? Every year I work as a Nurse, my job becomes increasingly more difficult. Every year someone adds one more step to what used to be a simple task. When an entire unit verbalizes dissatisfaction with a policy or procedure, does anyone say, "If every single one of you has a problem with this policy or procedure, we must rethink this policy or procedure"? No. What really happens is that the nurse manager says, "This was sent down by the powers that be and you will get over it eventually. You always do."

Well, the cat is out of the bag and no one wants to become a Nurse anymore. Because ultimately it doesn't matter how much they throw at you, you have to take it. Go get another job. Oh, that's right. The same governing bodies that made that rule oversee every hospital in America. The number of Nurses working within inpatient settings goes down each year. Which means the shortage is being felt greatest within the inpatient setting. Why are Nurses making the shift away from inpatient care? Read on.

Nurses need to document every policy, procedure, checklist, machine, and code that steals our time and mental energy. I truly do know what your thinking, "document *this* Curnayn." One more task on the already full plate. Well write it on a paper towel and then type it in an e-mail to me, because until someone compiles these so called *simple* tasks that steal our time and energy, nothing will change. Unfortunately telling people the system stinks is just not enough, unfortunately the every increasing shortage of Nurses does not paint a big enough picture for those at the top. No one will believe us until we have 100,000 thousand documented complaints about the same problem. Institutions want numbers and I suggest we give them exactly what they are looking for.

Just getting someone's blood sugar is an act of God. I used to be able to prick the person's finger and place a drop on a strip. Now I have to scan my badge, then scan the patient's bracelet, then scan the bottle that the strips come in, and then place the drop of blood on the strip. Better yet, I have to get certified yearly on how to use an accu check machine. My badge has been locked from accu check usage; I am currently an invalid user. I must take a test and then have someone from education unlock my badge thus allowing me the restricted right to get someone's blood sugar. Let's discuss the absurdity of making a Registered Nurse prove yearly she can obtain a blood sugar on a patient. Diabetic children as young as five years of age can obtain their own blood glucose but an adult Registered Nure must get checked yearly on this competency. I'm not feeling the professional image of Nursing our collegiate elite refer to. How very disrespectful and sad. I'm valued, right guys?

Now let's start really looking at all the steps that have been added to the hundred things we do everyday. Let's do some serious studies on how much time it takes to get an IV bag, medication, supplies, and linens. If you add something to my plate then it makes sense you need to take something away to even the work load, but to date the plate gets dumped on.

Recently, it was mandated that IV bags would no longer be sent up to the floors. We now have to make a phone call when we need one. Again, that alone doesn't seem all that awful, but I used to be able to run through the med room and grab the bag from a bin. So if I get caught up with, you know, actual patient care and forget to order the bag, it is just one more thing I have to do. But I'm sure we will save thousands and it is again one more task placed on the plate of the Nurse.

Standard operating procedure is that linen carts can **not** have the tarp up because of the potential of dust bunnies or germs getting on the linens. The carts in most institutions get switched out every twelve hours. With all the germs in the hospital, leaving the tarp up does what? I'll tell you what it does; it allows me to get linens quickly. But no, that can't be because someone, somewhere, said I must leave that tarp down. I asked for studies to prove this was a health issue, but none were provided. It seems so childish, but document the hundreds of other petty rules that have been applied to inpatient staff and you have a communist government in place. Those on the front line are helpless when it comes to machines, policies and checklists; you have no choice in the matter. Rule states tarp down!

When Nurses complain about a policy, the answer is, "This meets National Safety Standards." that is what someone more powerful then you states?

When a Nurse complains about staff personnel who don't function within their job description, the supervisor says, "I don't have the time and energy to document this problem." The person experiencing the problem doesn't have the authority to document it. Hence, there is no accountability of ancillary staff within a unit. A Nurse stated how bad the secretary she worked with was but then recanted how she was pretty good to "her". You mean for "her" patients, or for "her". That secretary neglected over half of the patients she was hired to serve and you're happy because she is pretty good to "you". That is what working on a floor has turned into; pretty soon Nurses will have to start carrying around cash to hand out tips. The nurse manager says, "I'll talk to them and gives them a gentle nudge in the right direction." Accountability ultimately falls in the lap of the Nurse.

Who says we really care about you and are willing to fight these battles for you? Who says we won't beat up on the Nurse anymore? Who says all this murmuring and complaining must amount to a valid complaint? Administration has allowed the system to crumble upon itself and now is wondering what happened.

The unspoken rule is "everyman for himself." If you have a network of friends on a given floor, it is manageable. But even with that support system, there are days Nurse go home shaking their heads. Why did I become a Nurse again? Maybe I should take the pay cut and move to outpatient or the education department.

When the institution I worked for began the transition to a new computer system, they asked me to attend computer training to help facilitate the process among my peers. When the training began, I heard more than one nurse say, "This is such a nice break from having to work as a nurse." One peer said, "I told my boss to sign me up for any special projects you might have working."

I have to say it was a nice break. Wow! I didn't want to go back to my "real" work. So this is how people get to spend their days at work. So to remove the stress, nurses choose to remove themselves from the bedside and turn to roles of education, advanced practice and management. There are many Nurses who have left jobs for lesser pay just to escape the environment they were in.

We have a Nursing shortage and I have one idea of how every hospital in America could help with this soon to become national crisis. Implement a policy that every nurse with a license work on the floor for a minimal of two days a month. That doesn't seem like much, but when you consider every licensed professional working in an institution, we will place a multitude of nurses back into the field. Just maybe in those two days a month, people who are in positions to help change the system will experience first hand what the problems are. Come on, guys. We have a soon to be national crisis here and time is not on our side. So what will be the response of those personnel when asked to put on a pair of scrubs and dust off their stethoscope? I venture to say the responses will go something like this

"It's not clinically safe for me to function as a nurse anymore; I've been out of the field for too long."

Place the above people on the simplest floor in the hospital, download the drug reference guide to their Blackberry and point out they are still in better shape than any nurse just coming out of college.

You'll hear: "I can't get the work I need to get done in my current position."

Well, welcome to my world. Everyday I go into work knowing I have to make decisions on who to serve first, my patients or my computer documentation. Not to mention the bombardment of requests from a million other sources.

You'll hear: "The reason I'm in this position is because I didn't like the job I was in."

Ahhh, now we're talking. You stepped out of the ranks because you didn't see how this war could be won, so you went AWOL and left your wounded and injured in the trenches. Well, we are still bleeding and helpless with no resolution in sight. Guess what, America? We are NOT encouraging our children to become nurses. So how will hospitals determine who gets the available inpatient beds? Hmmm. Gas lines of 1989. Just some thought-provoking moments.

"Teamwork" was the big buzz in corporate America ten years ago. Self- managed team, independent teams, facilitated teams; teams were to change the way business worked. Well, corporate America faces the same pitfalls it always had: every man clamoring to get to the illusive top. Nurses do need to work as teams. First and foremost, for the well-being of our patients, and secondly, we need to start changing the system. We need to tell the world what is wrong, but first, we have to figure it out ourselves. I spent many hours thinking on this subject before the actual problems began surfacing. I have just scratched the surface. I'm counting on every nurse in America to help. Let's start documenting (on paper towels) things that don't improve the quality of care we give our patients.

Many people have been singing the tune that unions are needed and many states have done just that. Historically unions start out with the interest of the people they represent as their first priority. Eventually they morph into political activist and lobbyist groups, which then makes it challenging to have the whole hearted interest of the population they represent. Politics and I don't meld; do what is right because it is right, but in politics everything is grey and I find that to be such a wretched color. You want more money, but yet you give it away with the hopes of yet another bureaucracy to change the system..

We hold the power. We just haven't tapped into that power. Start sending me your policies, procedures, checklists and complaints. Don't pay me dues because I'm hoping after we stop feeding the giants, maybe you will get more money. We need fewer bureaucracies. We've allowed people who don't actually touch a patient tell us what works and doesn't work, and hospitals have turned a deaf ear to the voice of the flesh and bones of an institution. People love the numbers; no one will be able to argue the documented complaints that come from Nurses across a nation. Now we are talking power. There are things we do every day that don't improve safety or quality of care we give our patients. Please e-mail MetoWeConsulting.com those non value added activities administration says to "just do" and the Nurse says "for what"?

Chapter Four

Merks Manual of Nursing Shortage

The nursing shortage is a symptom. Let's try to reflect on the disease process here and then touch on the all-so-detrimental symptoms that have ensued.

Disease
No Boundaries

Nursing has no boundaries; everyone can impose on a nurse. Every department calls the nurse to make sure the patient is ready so their schedule stays on track. So Nurses must always step out of their job description while the world around them has very defined boundaries. I go into detail about this in chapter six about team work. Does anyone ever check my schedule? Oh, that's right. I don't have one. Does anyone care that it's 15:00 and I haven't eaten lunch yet?

We get beat up by every Bully on the block, and when Bob Bully is done with us, our fellow nurses take a few blows to the face during report. But for a moment, let's focus on Mr. Bully and what he gets away with. Bob comes in the form of many departments, people and electronic devices. We receive phone calls from nearly every department in the hospital. The most common phone calls are from pharmacy, laboratory, radiology, and physicians. Are we in the middle of doing something else when these phone calls arrive? Of course we are. Does anyone ever think that a nurse must remains flexible for thirteen hours while almost everyone else keeps rules and time lines?

"I'm in the middle of mixing chemotherapy I can't answer the phone." That sounds reasonable. When can a Nurse in good conscience, not answer her phone that has been government issued at the beginning of the day? If you don't answer it, will someone be put out by the inconvenience? Yes, as a matter of fact, they will. What does the secretary do if she can't find the Nurse? Ask a peer or call the charge Nurse, and if they are busy, are they thrilled to take care of YOUR work. Some Nurses are notorious for shutting off their phones to avoid the bombardment. Can't say I blame them, but instead of being passive-aggressive about the issue, let's hash it out and find a better solution.

Nursing has no boundaries; everyone else seems to have a point at which they can go home. This is a classic scenario: I have been just slammed with meds to chart, notes to write, orders to verify, reports to give, and a patient needs the bed-side commode at 19:10. The dreaded hour. Whose responsibility is it to tend to this patient? In my experience, the above falls on the lap of the nurse. The nurse works well past 19:30, while all those around her have long since left.

Disease
Money-saving Coke machines—I mean crucial
medical supplies

Many hospitals are implementing machines that dispense everything from medications to toothbrushes. Does this machine save those units money? They sure do. Do those machines decrease job satisfaction of staff? They sure do. Do those machines steal valuable time from Nurses that could be spent at the bedside? They sure do. With the state of health care in such a crisis, does executive staff love employees who save them money? They sure do.

This machine is just one more thing that steals my time from the bedside and decreases the quality of care I give my patients. But no one can quantitatively break down what I do as a Nurse. No one knows how to bill for the services of a Nurse. But when money-saving gadgets are implemented, does anyone really consider the cost to patient care?

Medication dispensing machines were sold to hospitals with the sales pitch of saving money and decreasing medication errors. They definitely save the institution money, but the numbers are indicating they may be increasing medication errors.

A new report from the U.S. Pharmacopeia (USP) reveals that hospital medication errors may be on the increase despite efforts to combat the problem. The report is based on an analysis of medication errors submitted to the USP's tracking system, known as MEDMARX.

In all, the USP received 192,477 reports of medication errors from the 482 hospital and health care facilities using the system in 2002. Reported errors had increased by 82% over the previous year. The increase, it must be said, may not necessarily indicate that current hospital drug safety efforts are failing; it may only mean that participating hospitals are getting better at identifying and reporting medication mistakes. Such a possibility confounds the interpretation of results.

USP acknowledges that new technologies, such as computerized prescriber order entry, and automated dispensing devices, have the potential to improve safety. But the new report shows that such technologies can "also introduce unforeseen errors that may not have been present previously."[11]

During this study from 2002 to 2003, an 82% increase in reported errors occurred. Despite machines and checklists medication errors continue to be on the rise. This study does not address Nursing medication errors but I propose the more you stress out Nurses, the more medication errors there will be, and yet the system continues to dump more on our lap each month. We need an overhaul of the whole system. If it doesn't directly improve the quality of the care I give my patient, take it off my plate.

Technology must be improved upon and be held accountable to the standards of excellent care. If the drug dispensing machine has added 30 minutes to the tasks I do in the day, processors and Nurses need to work diligently until that time comes down to at least 15 minutes. But currently the only cost being accounted for is the dollar and with that mentality, no one can give good care.

Disease
Unrealistic Policies
Chasm between reality and ideal

I have heard a room full of Nurses overtly express their dissatisfaction with a policy, only to be told this procedure is not up for discussion and we must keep national safety standards. If we wish to remain accredited and continue to receive our Medicare funding. How can hundreds of nurses dislike a policy and no one in administration be willing to fight the fight? There has to be a better way. Nurses don't always implement the procedure the way it is written. We must, in the course of a day, place our licenses on the line because we don't follow the dictated policy. Don't tell me you care. Show me by fighting just an occasional battle for me. If you haven't noticed, I'm diligently taking care of your product/customer, or, more importantly, patients who have names, lives, children, experiences, and yes, they are sick. While I do that for this organization, can someone support me, can someone say that this policy is too time-consuming and unrealistic, can someone say I will put on a pair of scrubs and get my hands dirty?

Quality improvement is the primary source of cost reduction, but if you can't engage your employees to see the overall mission of the institution, you are doomed. Again, the mission of every hospital in the world is to give compassionate and excellent medical care. Consultants in suits don't talk our language and will never be able to effectively engage the front line of hospitals. Their cost-cutting measures seem logical on paper and their thinking streamlined while discussing the issues from board rooms.

This would be an interesting experiment. Have someone who knows policy follow a real Nurse around for a day, ensuring everything is done according to policy, and let's document the findings from both perspectives. Talk about a revolution. People would be forced to look at the hard cold facts from both sides of the fence. I'm just brainstorming guys. People love to tell me, "that is not realistic." Well, statistics say we will be short over 1 million Nurses by 2020. Is that realistic? The issue of unreasonable policies has been boiling since I graduated in 1991. When the administration ignores the obvious chasm between the implementation and the written, to me it means they don't really care, or, at the very least, don't know what to do with results when they get them. But by **not** acknowledging this obvious fact leaves Nurses with a feeling that no one really cares how difficult their job is. Not to mention the license she places in jeopardy every time a policy is not followed as written.

Let's look at rewriting the policy to be safe while more efficient. Oh, that's right. We have to write policy that looks good to a higher power (it's not God, but close). Does this governing body have to worry about the harsh reality of actually implementing the care to the patients? You know, those patients they claim they are so desperately trying to protect. I view this God-like figure in our lives as the overbearing mother who won't let her child ride his bike unless in full football gear for fear something may happen. So many things we do cannot be placed on a piece of paper or electronically documented, and every time a new documentation requirement is placed before us, we are taken away from the bedside. Every minute you take a Nurse away from the bedside is a decrease in job satisfaction, patient satisfaction, and quality of care. So what are we going to do about it? Create more checklists?

These are just two examples of mismanaged authority regarding Nursing processes. Let me preface these statements by stating that every Nurse from every hospital in America can give me at least one example of a story similar to these.

This is a prime example of administration not listening. We had a policy on how to administer insulin (it was rarely followed as written). Nurses continually reported on the overbearing nature of the policy. We got new computers and the nursing staff in the computer class said this process of checking insulin was just too arduous. They basically told us, this is what they devised to meet National Safety Standards and you have to implement it this way. This was how safe implementation of insulin looks like. Well, that's great, but it's just one more thing that removes me from actually caring for my patient. Maybe someone can explain to them why they haven't seen me.

Who was that policy written for, the patient, a lawyer, or maybe a governing body? We were told insulin was the most reported medication error in hospitals, which is why they defended their position on the subject. Insulin overdose can be fatal, and administering it should not be taken lightly. Look at individualized errors and you will find behind the scenes a stressed out Nurse who had too much on her plate. The cause of the error is where the solution lies, so the Nurse lost her license for the grave mistake of "killing someone" and a more stringent policy is written. How many policies are there, that are improbable at best and impossible on most days to implement as written? This topic alone could create a revolution. We all know the policy doesn't decrease errors but shifts the liability away from the hospital and onto the Nurse. Every time a policy is not followed as written the Nurse places her license on the line. So Nurses continue to look for the balance between policy and efficiently, effectively and safely taking care of our patients.

When I graduated Nursing care plans were implemented, which didn't improve the quality of care I gave the patient at all. I worked in one institution that said you had to chart a progress note on each patient daily (more realistic action for determining a plan of care—at least you could read what occurred during that day). Hospital standards sometimes come in the form of checklists, and having a plan of care was on that list. Doctors document daily their action and plan, but that was not enough. Whatever the case, a form was created (thousands spent), education given on the form (thousands spent again), time spent filling out the form (wasted). Spending 5 minutes at the bedside with your patient (priceless). I feel like a MasterCard commercial. It fulfilled a necessary requirement given to us by the greater powers that exist in the Land of Oz It was supposed to be a multi-disciplinary form for all departments to chart on, but that didn't happen on a regular basis.. Nursing was primarily responsible for ensuring the form was completed, even though it did not increase patient safety, patient satisfaction or improve patient care. It simply met a checklist standard.

The above is just one of many examples of processes that don't fulfill the bigger purpose. Who do we serve? Who has to fight the powers that be? No one can afford not to listen anymore. We don't like our jobs and we don't recommend our children take on the profession. You want to hire a guy in a suit, bring a bulldog to listen to complaints of nursing and then have that bulldog start fighting whoever needs to be fought to get things changed.

Disease
Every Man for himself

I had difficulty determining if this was a disease process or just a symptom of a problem. With much reflection, I have concluded it was and has been a problem since Adam and Eve. From day one when Eve brought that apple to Adam, it has been every man for himself. Adam's reply to God was, "It was that woman you gave to me." Threw her right under the bus.

Women are the loving, nurturing, caretakers of a family from the beginning of time. We nurse our children; we nurse people back to health. To nurse is an action of well-being, an action to make the recipient well-nourished or physically better. Well, now it holds the title of both noun and verb. People live longer and people get sicker. Technology has made nursing a medical specialty far beyond what Florence Nightingale could have ever imagined.

When you are not pressed in on all sides, it is much easier to be loving, kind, professional, and compassionate. Although the pressures of Nursing brought the "every man for himself" problem to the surface, it remains a basic instinctual act of self preservation. We must rise above ourselves to look for the good of everyone (patient care assistant, secretary, nurse, pharmacist, laboratory, nutrition services, and don't forget the patient) versus finding the "work around" to alleviate our own stresses.

So let's review. If I care to too much I won't have all my i's dotted, which will result in interrogation from the incoming nurse. If I care too much I get the privilege of staying late, while all those who took a narrower approach to inpatient care get to go home.. If I care too much, my emotions allow me to dislike this job, which I need to pay the mortgage. If I care too much, I get angry with the perceived injustices, and the question is, what do I do with this anger?

Symptom
Job Dissatisfaction (Anger/Apathy)

Getting angry as a Nurse is just that: unresolved anger that goes nowhere. Best case scenario: I'm going to my nurse manager. I have a valid complaint/injustice with which I'm seeking problem resolution. The nurse manager listened intently and then consulted her core staff, who have been around for at least five to twenty-five years. I like to refer to the core staff as the good ol' boys. They watch each other's back and could run the floor with their eyes closed. They don't have a big problem with the current situation. In the mind of the nurse manager, and with the advent of the Nursing shortage only worsening, she must keep happy and ultimately retain the core group. Remember now, seasoned nurses have learned to deal with stress by making their circumstances somewhat more bearable.

How can one really experience the joy of serving others in an environment with the unspoken rule, "every man for himself"? We go through the motions as described by our job description, but when pressed to the limits of our own abilities, we shut down, get angry, and eventually turn to apathy. So we hear stories of Nurses talking at the Nurses station while those around them, patient care techs, secretaries, and fellow peers are slammed with work. Apathy, to me, is the ultimate pain killer to all that ails a person. The numbing effect lessens the sound of the phone, call button or disgruntled family member. Apathy is a hundred times more addicting than oxycontin. Just open your windows and listen to the world. Nurses see others not bothered by the needs around them. The first thought is, no one else seems to be upset, why should I be? What is that drug you take to help get through the day? "Oh, Apathy, you call it. How can I get myself some of that?"

Day after day I experience the same frustrations with no resolution in sight. Working hard to do what is right, for what? The angel on my left shoulder tells me my reward is in heaven and my patients are blessed by my high work ethic combined with compassionate care. The devil on my right shoulder tells me the frustration and stress is going to cause me a heart attack (no one appreciates you anyway) and it's just not worth the aggravation.

Is it worth the aggravation? Hence the punch in and punch out mentality. I go in, do the best I can under the circumstance, and punch out. My conscience is clear. I can't change the situation. I neither have the strength, resources or the desire to change this situation any more. So is the answer recognition? Should our reward be here on earth because waiting for that one in heaven is just not going to cut it? Recognition doesn't take away my daily stress of the job. Administration seems to think by telling us how much they appreciate us or by giving presents, we won't mind the hundred things that frustrate the hell out of us. So many nurses entered the field for all the right reasons. If we could just give staff a glimmer at the end of the tunnel. The system is going to change and it is going to happen from the inside out. Everyone reading this who is committed to the call of service could be the first in history to change the face of in-patient care.

You want to understand the heart of a nurse? Catch him or her right at the point of anger, because only at that point is there hope of saving the heart. The anger indicates there is still emotion enough to provoke a response. Because apathy follows quickly after the anger, especially when no hope of change can be found on the horizon. People seek marriage counselors when they feel something, even if it is just unadulterated anger. Those marriages that have slipped into apathy don't have a chance. They just go through the motions until the husband or wife comes home one day and says, "I'm leaving." Everyday, nurses say, "I'm leaving." Rumor has it there is a two-to-four year average for new graduate nurses within the inpatient settings.

Symptom
All the work must be done on the preceding shift

Does anything in the inpatient world actually occur according to schedule? If it does, I have yet to experience it. So we as nurses expect and demand that the nurse before us have all the work done, knowing full well that somehow putting in a two-minute peripheral IV sometimes turns into a thirty-five minute job. The trip to the bathroom turned out to be a full bath and linen change. Oh yeah, explain why you were so busy. No love coming from this nurse. I want to know why the work is not done. Triaging means taking the most important life threatening issues and moving our way down the list.

On one floor I worked, a nurse stated if the patient arrived to the floor before 6:00 p.m., the paper work and orders for the admission was the complete responsibility of the previous shift. In other words, don't pass on any work that should have been done on your shift. The hospital is open 24 hours a day, but we as nurses expect and demand that the patient and all the implementation of care be in a neat present with a tidy little bow on it.

Every nurse on the floor has been a victim of a day gone bad. Is it the fault of the preceding shift nurse? I don't believe so. But to ensure we have a good day, we interrogate and demand every single aspect of that shift's care be done before the preceding nurse can go home. At least we start out in the most perfect environment. I have seen nurses give someone a hard time about a kardex (brief written summary of the patient) not being filled out, and then talk for at least twenty minutes with their bud. This is a little hard to swallow after thirteen hours of service. So why are we not nice to each other?

Generally speaking, are Nurses lazy? No, the lazy Nurse is the exception, not the rule. We have been conditioned to believe it must all be done; **not** for the sake of the patient but for fear of reprisal of the oncoming shift. We go crazy trying to ensure *it* is all done. A Nurse just the other day said, "We were raised to think this way." This statement speaks volumes.

The disciplines involved with patient care are pharmacy, laboratory, central supply, dietary, patient care technician, secretaries and respiratory therapist. What time do these people punch out? What time is their shift over? Does the work they have get passed on to the next shift, or are they expected to get all **their** work done before punching out? Generally speaking, all of the above can count on their shift being over at a given time. The circumstance that may cause them to stay beyond that time would be occasional.

Symptom
We are not nice to each other

Remember, getting tough is the true nature of the game. How tough is tough enough, and who do we get tough with? Fellow nurses, employees, or the patients? I think in the process of getting tough you have to choose one of the above. Fortunately, nurses are the hardest on one another, which tells me there remains a heart of compassion for the patients. You only have to get wounded a few times before you learn to avoid that affliction again. How do we tap into that heart of compassion? Learn again that our fellow Nurses are not our foe but friend.

Pharmaceutical reps have often experienced much of the same tenacity when trying to pitch a drug to Nursing staff. I have asked reps over the years, their opinions on Nurses, and the most commonly used word is tough. It took many years to get that tough and I'm not letting my armor down for some floofy executive from the top who sends in his teams of experts.

Why are Nurse are so Tough?

James Carville, *Buck Up, Suck Up*

> The lesson here is that the battle does not always go to the biggest or the strongest. Especially in a fast-paced, ever-changing environment, the winner is going to be the person with the greatest flexibility. Flexibility confounds and confuses your adversaries and builds a sense of self confidence that you can handle anything they throw at you.[12]

Well no one can deny Nurses get a great deal thrown at them and suck it up. Gumby pales to our flexibility. This is just one reason why Nurses are self assured and confident. So when a pharmaceutical rep, physician or a consultant approaches them, they have the assuredness of a panther. You! Yeah, I'm talking to you! You really think you know more about this job? Then let me test your knowledge base. Let me see how you can remotely gain my respect and trust. Let's see how you handle a little opposition. Who understands the heart of a Nurse? That's right. A Nurse and only a Nurse. We win the small battles in hand-to-hand combat, but our elusive enemy continues to gain ground. To date, no one has a national, strategic plan that addresses our environment within the everyday work place.

I will stereotype three types of Nurses to give report to, because shift change is where a great deal of the stresses get acted out verbally. Let's classify the *perfect* Nurse to give report to, the friendly, helpful nurse who gets report kindly, tells you things that were beyond your scope of knowledge, and willingly follows through with any unresolved issues. I can hear the laughter. This is not the person we usually give report to.

The second kind is the *stoic,* quiet, generally disgusted-looking individual who wasn't happy upon her arrival and becomes increasingly unhappy with each and every second that passes after she punches in. Uhm, ok, whatever (which means I'll fix that after you leave). This individual glares and in a very pervasive manner tries to make you feel as small and insignificant as humanly possible. Did you get this done? Do you have everything ready for his procedure tomorrow at 3:00 p.m.? "Well, no, I don't. Do you possibly think you can follow through with that?" Argh. God bless the individual that doesn't allow herself to get sucked into this mind game. I remember asking one nurse, why are you so unpleasant? I wanted to scream, "I didn't do anything to you. I worked thirteen long hours. I took good care of my patients, and now all I want to do is go home." Did you know if you look mean enough, no one bothers you? It's really quite a good tactic. Everyone, including the patient, is so taken back by the disposition that no one bothers this person.

The *know-it-all* nurse: she is an expert in every bodily function and lab value that has ever been seen to the medical world. Brilliant Nurses of this nature, and they really are brilliant, can go either way. If their self-esteem is low, they must point out the deficiency of everyone around them, which makes giving report difficult. Although this nurse is generally less abrasive to me, generally speaking they are very well versed in many topics and especially knowledgeable in their chosen area. If you cordially agree to all the important information they give you, change of shift/report is relatively easy. Thank you so much. I didn't even think of that. Yes, that was just brilliant. Compared to our stoic type, the personality is generally much more pleasant and, 99% of the time, they truly are excellent nurses, which makes their overbearing demeanor all that more tolerable.

The symptoms are why the Nursing shortage rages. The disease processes have existed for over twenty years and could have been dealt with and addressed years ago. When the vise (increase in tasks/documentation) was first placed on us, we said,

"Okay, I can do that." And then it just got tighter and tighter. We had a stretch of time when lawyers ran rampant, making millions from mistakes — and many were bona fide mistakes. My question is, were those mistakes the exception or the rule, and did we go crazy setting up checks and balances for the exception? There is a balance here, because safe patient care can never be compromised. But until you have robots implementing the care, there will always be human error. So let's just stress Nurses out more by placing increased demands on them. That should lower medication errors. This is Physiology 101. Has anyone looked at the disease that caused the impending Nursing shortage?

Now let's shift gears. We have all been the victim of a day gone bad. You punched in at 07:00. The next chance you have to breathe, it is 14:00 and no real sign of a break in sight. Remember, that was just a breath you took at 14:00. If you go to lunch, who will get all your paper and computer charting done? And if you don't do it now, you will be even further behind upon your arrival back. Now my poor patients are just going to have to understand their basic needs are the last thing on my triage list.

We all started out with the real intent of helping people. So what happened? Nurses, generally speaking, are not nice to each other. WHY? When we first got into the field, we just wanted to be able to function like the experienced nurse with no one hovering over us quizzing our every move. If your preceptor says you're a train wreck, you don't get the job. So everyone endures and tries to make nicey nice with the person holding her future in the palm of his hand. Not to mention we spent all this time and money getting this education. We can't fail now. "Oh please, Lord, help me just endure and get through this." I believe this is the prayer of every believer and non-believer starting as a nurse still under the direction of a preceptor.

So this is the reality for the new nurse. You get to work at 0630 because you're so damn nervous and you're sure there is an extra lab value you might find. You must account for your every move, review each patient with your preceptor, and diligently get quizzed on every medication for all your patients. This task get easier as times goes on. When I precepted, I taught the new grad every bit of information stored in my little head, in increments so I didn't overwhelm her. After a few weeks of training I would quiz the grad on the information given.

The trend today is to quiz first and teach later. Does anyone like not having the answer? For example, I decided I needed a new challenge after spending ten years on an acute medical oncology floor. Critical care was the logical next step. I went into my training an excellent nurse, great assessment skills with a wonderful bedside manner. Well, no amount of time could have prepared me for this setting. I expected to get taught cardiac critical care. Instead, I attended classes and was expected to know the information upon arrival. I personally learn while implementing.

Our initial introduction to Swan Ganz catheters, of course, was in the class room, which moved to bedside. First time at bedside, I was quizzed on each line and all the dynamics of preload, afterload, and general heart functioning. Teach me once at the bedside, and then quiz me next time. Let me hear the information in the clinical setting with the equipment, monitors and numbers all at the learning field. In the ICU setting, just learning how to use the monitors is an achievement.

I hear crazy stories of preceptors pulling rank on grads. Why is this allowed to go on? I'll tell you why—because no one stops them and because the preceptee can't report such abuses. No new preceptee will win by complaining about their preceptor. Which, of course, didn't stop me. My fellow peers kept telling me to suck it up and keep my mouth shut. Of course, you know I didn't do that either. So we learn very early in out careers to suck it up and move on.

One story started out with a preceptor asking her student to check the compatibilities of the solutions that were infusing together through a Y site. The new grad, already under a tremendous amount of pressure, made the decision to start her day out with her primary responsibilities. I forgot to mention the above had been hanging for over 48 hours, which lead her to prioritize her day with morning assessments and medications. Well, well, well. Two hours later the preceptor comes to her and asks if she called pharmacy to check on the compatibilities, and she said, "No, I haven't yet.".

The all-knowing preceptor then informs her of her grave mistake. The solutions were not compatible and she placed the patient in danger. Why? I ask. Why? There are so, so many facts that nurses know just because they have been around a long time, little nuggets of information about tests, drugs and diseases that are primarily learned through experience. SHARE that knowledge with the younger nurses.

Symptom:
Amnesia; Labor Pains Theory

No one can understand the mind of a nurse except the Nurse. That labor pains theory again. For whatever reason, once Nurses leave the bedside they seem to forget. I worked with a Nurse who was getting her practitioners license and hadn't worked our floor in six months. She scheduled herself three days to work over spring break. The first day, she said something about us complaining too much. By the third day, she was verbalizing how happy she was that she wasn't going to be doing this anymore. Do what, I ask? When people leave the everyday stress of being a Nurse they forget how taxing it is—or maybe they just don't want to remember. They remember being frustrated with the system, but can't recall the exact reason for not wanting to be a floor nurse any longer.

To solidify my theory on Labor Pains. Try to take yourself back to the days your children were babies. This example applies more to women, but here I go. Do you remember how you felt when you got to leave the house without children in tow? Just starting the car, a sense of euphoria came over you, all alone, no chance of any child throwing a cheerio from the back seat at you. Diaper bag and bottles at home with Dad (not that you didn't make sure anything he would need was at his disposal). Ahhh, I might just drive around because this moment is just so peaceful.

When you have friends with little babies, do you tell yourself, "I should really see if I could watch those kids for an hour, just to see if she would like to get out of the house"? We can so vividly remember the above experience, but yet don't seem to reach out as often as maybe we should. Why don't we? I think, until reminded, we tuck those memories away. It wasn't horrible, but definitely a lot of work. We tend to reflect on the memories of joyful times, as we should. Babies are so beautiful and precious, but thank God they are only little for a season

Now let's reflect on nursing. The season never ends. We endure with no real hope of it getting better, so we create ways to alleviate stress. I have spoken to so many Nurses who have left the bedside and stated they could never do that again. The rhetorical question, do what? I worked with a charge Nurse who did allow herself to feel and see the needs of her staff. You could see the stress on her face. I saw her feel my stressors, but I never saw her trying to find solutions to those stressors. Why? I don't know, except that maybe she had absolutely no idea on how to change it. I believe she thought it must be just her. "I'm just out of practice in this role. Everyone doesn't feel this way day after a day." She worked as charge *maybe* one day a week. You can do anything for one day a week. When you are not in the middle of the fire, you forget how hot it gets. Administration doesn't want to *feel* a situation they can't fix anymore than we do.

So let's review. Nurses are the smartest, toughest, most caring, strong-willed, hard-working, stressed, selfless, difficult, compassionate bunch of people you will ever meet. That's a cocktail that needs a drink named after it. When we punch out of the environment, Nurses know how to have a good time. We play the best practical jokes, we have the best time at any party, we make the most lowest-maintenance wives. We are programmed to suck it up, so we take real life in strides. It really is a great life lesson. Any time I want to whine about my life, I just go into work and am reminded of my blessings.

Nurses have been accused of not being professional. Which may hold some truth. With all due respect, we accomplish more in the course of a day than most. When we have a patient die, we don't have the leisure to not take care of the other four patients. At least when business employees land a big client, your boss takes you out for dinner and a few drinks. Our importance is huge. We (with the help of staff and our unseen advisor) affect the outcomes of people's lives in far reaching ways. Yet, we also take the role of servant, and as practitioner, we take on jobs that would be considered the lowest of the low, yet we hold ourselves to a high degree of medical knowledge. We truly beat each other and ourselves up if we miss a diagnosis (the fact we didn't go to medical school is irrelevant). Okay, we all know nursing is not a glamorous job, but is that the reason for the shortage? Partly, but I suggest the problem runs far deeper than this.

Is corporate America professional? Let's just say we need to define this statement. Nursing is at least overt about their aggression and frustration. Usually the knife comes directly at you, and with precision, I must say. Corporate America would be smart to eliminate the cc/bcc on every computer. It is used to pass gossip along the greased bureaucratic railroad. Everyone has to cover their ass. How many subjects have managers been involved in just because they were cc'd on the subject? If you were hired to do the job, please just do it. If I don't need the information to do my job effectively, don't send it to me. I personally will not tolerate the above crap. I always want an open door policy, but my goodness, the mass of e-mails that middle management gets just so everyone can be informed, is ridiculous. No wonder nursing management can't effectively make changes.

The more stresses you place on me in the course of a day, the more unprofessional I become. Everyone has a breaking point, and nursing as a profession has met it. Nurses either verbally attack one another or just check out mentally. Well we can't attack the patients (they are sick, for God's sake), so we dispense a little of our attitude to those around us.

Chapter Five

War Room
Inside look into a Nursing unit

O ur environment profoundly affects our person. When we see children living in the ghetto surrounded by violence, crime and drugs, people expect the sins of the environment to reveal themselves in the next generation. And as history has proven, the cycle repeats itself unless the environment changes. I have read few articles that mentioned the environment within Nursing, and the ones that did briefly mentioned the subject with such political correctness it was a slap in the face.

High control with high support = great environment

High control with low support = Nursing environment

The cycle repeats itself unless the environment changes. So what is being done in our Nursing environment to ensure we produce happier Nurses? I've seen bonuses, lots of verbal praise, and gift certificates. The big buzz lately seems to be we need to let our nurses know we appreciate them, and I think they know administration is genuinely trying. I worked with Nurse of the year (of that institution) one day. Of course we all know she is a phenomenal nurse and a team player; otherwise, there is no way she would have received such an award. She was having a terrible day. It was written all over her face. I wanted to help but of all the specialties I float to, I was least comfortable in that one. I offered what I could. When the day began to settle down, I asked her what could have made this day better. We all know she was appreciated with honors, gifts, and photos that were publicly displayed throughout the hospital. She mumbled something about being paid more for her efforts. Increased pay does not equal increased job satisfaction. It helps to endure the pain, but the pain still exists. We can honor and appreciate nurses all day long, but if the environment doesn't change, they still go home weary and frustrated.

If our environment is bad, we buy into the wrong things. How many inpatient staff throw their hands up (metaphorically speaking) and says "it's not my problem"? When looking for problems and resolutions, we often look to the most outspoken individual. To get to the root of this problem, we need to implore the heart of the silent Nurse as well. Many Nurses that I have had the greatest respect for over the years are often the quiet ones who blend into the woodwork. They have not lowered their personal standard, but they also can't invest energy into the people or the place they work in. If you ask this person for anything, they graciously will assist, but they don't actively search out helping others, for the sake of self preservation.

I graduated in 1991, at which time only eight-hour shifts were available. We couldn't wait for twelve-hour shifts so we could work only three days a week, allowing us greater freedom to go on vacation or just enjoy our family. Well, I'm not sure the latter of those things necessarily took place in the world of nursing. Many nurses chose to work a fourth shift, making their work week 48 hours. Which, I guess isn't bad, except for the fact that you leave the house at 6:15 on average and get home at 8:00. This time frame applies to both day and night shifts. On the days I worked, I was of no use to my family. I came home spent, emotionally and physically, after a day of service-oriented work.

Would Nurses be happier doing eight hour shifts versus twelve? I believe so. I know I am much happier doing eight hours. Say I was contemplating calling in sick, if I knew it was an eight-hour shift, I'd say "I can make it for 8 hours". The twelve-hour is a little bit more ominous, causing me to make the sick call. Possible solutions: allow Nurses the option to call in for the last four hours.

Nurses are hired for an hourly wage to take care of the physical and emotional needs of two-to-six patients for a twelve hour period. One hospital

I worked for paid med surg nurses and ICU nurses on the same pay scale. With one respect, that seems unfair because of the knowledge base needed to be an ICU nurse, but on the other hand, there is not an ICU nurse out there who wants to go back to being a med surg nurse. This is where people need to start speaking the truth. Why would you never want to go back to med surg nursing? Don't worry, tell me the truth, no one from administration is here.

Working on the floors is physically and psychologically stressful. You feel like a beat-down dog by the end of the day. ICU nurses do experience stress, life and death, and yes, that can be stressful. But those who love ICU also love the adrenaline and expertise of it all. Stressful but yet exhilarating.

Floor nurses get great satisfaction for a job well done. They have excellent assessment skills and proactive thinking regarding the needs of the patient. Who are better nurses? Well, we all know the answer to that one. We cannot survive without each other, so when an ICU nurse is getting report from the floor, don't hammer her with questions. If people didn't crash and burn on occasion the ICU Nurse would be out of a job and we already determined that ICU Nurse doesn't want to work on the floors. Get what you can get during report and be compassionate. If you honestly feel the nurse that gave you report bordered on incompetence, do something about it. Give her a call later and start the conversation out like this, "Hey, Lisa, wanted to give you an update on Mr. Smith. I know how stressful it is to have a patient go bad. I'm calling to let you know some things that

I as the receiving nurse need to know when getting a crashing patient."

Come on, guys. The med surg Nurse was a nervous wreck. Let's start giving each other a break, let the beatings stop. Will the med surg Nurse accept the helpful advice with a willing spirit? We can only hope. Will the ICU Nurse get down from her pedestal and see all Nurses as equals?

Work Ethics

A person's true self worth is internalized. The internal aggravation reminds me that I continue to remain a person of worth. When I let go of the standard that caused my soul to grieve is when I lose that worth. The victories we have won for ourselves pass, but the victories we have achieved helping others have a much more lasting effect on our own self worth. The accomplishments of Nurses are many and their knowledge invaluable. But knowing more facts and figures than our peers doesn't increase our self worth in the long haul. Our accomplishments make us feel great, especially at the moment of achieving them, but then we must go on to the next one to get that same great feeling again. We are truly never happy until we learn to serve others. So when each nurse is asked what her fondest memory of being a nurse is, it will always be when she truly served her patients and made a difference. To date, I have not heard one person mention it was her own awesome abilities.

So we are back to the same dilemma. The system does not allow us to serve our patients first. Work ethics are defined by the person working. For some, calling in sick once a month is an acceptable standard; for others, once a year is more than the average.

I worked every Saturday afternoon my entire junior and senior year in high school. I remember asking off for the prom, worrying if they were going to give me the day off. My mom obviously overdid that work ethic thing. After years of service at the grocery store, I realized others didn't hold the same standard I did. What transpired is a serious value shift. I looked back on my years of dedicated service and said no more. I called in sick. I didn't show up when I was scheduled (by accident), and no longer invested in the quality of work I gave. I was so scared when I realized I hadn't showed up for a scheduled day, but I soon realized there were no tangible consequences for my action. This was a regularly occurring event with kids working there. Caring gets me what? The first store I worked for started non-college bound employees out at higher pay than those who had been with them for years.

Eventually, I just didn't invest any commitment to that corporation. My definition of work ethic based on minimal standards. Get to work on time, perform a job/task paid or unpaid to the best of the persons ability or at the very least work during the designated hours for which the person has verbally or contractually agreed upon. Notice I said at the very least. Does every institution have employees who believe they should get paid to stand around? Are there employees who seem to be incognito for indefinite periods of time? You stand there looking for someone to get ice water for a patient, make a phone call, or just help turn a patient, but no one is around. You can't have team work it you don't have strong work ethics. So you can't force an ethic into people, and in that case, there needs to be external levels of accountability.

Just recently a secretary told me she was on hold for fifteen minutes and I would have to call myself. The secretary came into the patient's room while I was caring for him and gave me her announcement that she was not going to sit on hold; it was now my problem. I pointed out that I was diligently taking care of the patient and that when her work was finished she could try again and when mine was finished I would be more than happy to make the phone call. We can't allow those who take down the team to flourish.

We need to start building working relationships where everyone benefits from working hard in a functional environment—strong work ethics (based on the attributes of a servant) combined with team building.

In the words of Oswald Chambers

> "The man who has been dulled by sin will say that he is not even conscious of it."[13]

Lowering the standard creeps up on the most devoted in patient staff. "I can't stress myself about things that are out of my control." I must focus on that which I can control. The things staff can control /manipulate are assignments, discharges, admissions, and who becomes charge nurse and who does not. I have seen the dearest, sweetest people ignore call lights, phones and family members within a foot of them. If presented with the facts of what they have just chosen to ignore, they would give a string of statements indicating they would never get home if they worried about and tended to ALL the needs around them.

Which leads right back to the genre of "Well, look around you. Do you see anyone else tending to/ perceiving the needs around them?" If I try to raise the standard of my work environment, **my** patients won't get the care they need. Notice I bolded the **my**, because we diligently try to take care of our own patients. We hold the standard high for ourselves, which is why we hear such wonderful stories of great Nurses and the service they give.

But that is not what this book is about. This book is about a system that has broken all the rules of fair play. Actually, there are no rules except the unspoken rule that the Nurse is held accountable to facilitate and implement all care of the patient. If a doctor missed something, the Nurse should have seen it. To add insult to injury. Nurses have to legally dot all the i's of this day, which means documenting on every checklist and computer to the letter of the law. First and foremost, our patients will look good on paper and our report will be thorough. The hospital must look good to those accrediting bodies, and when the paperwork looks good, we look good.

What motivates people to take pride in their work? I propose motivation comes from the hope that they can achieve the outcomes that give them a feeling of pride and satisfaction.

Work is defined here as outcomes achieved at the work place; both measurable and non-measurable outcomes.

Can we as Nurses achieve the outcomes as described below?

Outcomes

1. Patient is happy with the care they receive
2. Patient received top notch medical care and implementation from all departments (we as Nurses are the hub that makes this wheel turn)
3. We feel professionally satisfied with our jobs
4. The unit functions as a team, with everyone looking to the needs of all the patients on a given unit.
5. I will be able to care for my patients needs today.

Have your Nursing unit come up with four outcomes they would like to see from the work they do.

If there is no hope of achieving those outcomes. There is no hope of motivating your staff.

What is the goal of any one person's job in the hospital, every single employee, even the techno dudes locked up in the basement somewhere?

Excellent patient care.

Chapter Six

Nursing Units Shouldn't that mean teamwork?

Who has the right to have an easy day? The secretary, nurse, patient care assistant or nurse manager? We all filled out an application and agreed to work for a set hourly wage. It absolutely floors me that some people feel their job is limited to a few simple tasks. The nurse manager is salaried, but unfortunately has often opted out of floor nursing and thought management was the next step, only to realize that it also is plagued with its own set of difficulties. How about trying to make our current work situation better? Some floors function better than others but the problems that exist are the same on every unit, just varying degrees. Functioning as a unit means if one person has no work to finish, they look toward their peers and see how everyone else is doing.

Upper management wants to make patient satisfaction ratings increase, but no one is in the trenches
to actually make things better. Upper management
spend their days in meetings. Accountability is a
self governed attribute with unit functioning. If your
work ethic is low no one within a unit will hold you
accountable to a higher standard. Every man for
himself!

In the book *The Leadership Pill,* Blanchard and
Muchnick describes profit.

> "Profit is the applause you get for taking care
> of your customers and creating a motivating
> environment for people".[13]

So the applause a Nurse gets is not profit or gain,
but the satisfaction of a job well done. The environment is not exactly what one would call motivating.
For the believer you have the assurance that our
heavenly Father has promised to reward you.

So I should serve knowing my reward is in
heaven? Yes, you should and we probably would
continue to serve without overt recognition if the
system allowed us to do just that, but that currently is
an unreality. I don't mind not getting the overt recognition as much as I mind not having the support of
the employees who are also being paid to also serve
the patients.

What does it mean to function as a unit? Hospitals
all over the United States have named a location of a
hospital followed by unit. Cardiac critical care unit,

oncology unit, maternity unit, pediatric unit. Who, what and where did this unit transpire from, because I surely haven't seen it. Truly there lies the solution the Holy Grail—the undiscovered magical place to work. The place that actually functions as a unit.

The expression one bad apple ruins the barrel holds so true. One member of the unit staff that doesn't function as a team can take down the morale of so many. My areas of greatest frustration are not with serving my patients, but in dealing within a framework that does not realize that every hospital employee serves the patient. Nurses are the point of service, but we depend on many, many, other people to implement our jobs effectively. Who stocks the linen cart, the med room, the clean utility, empties the linens or keeps the computers virus free and working effectively? Hospitals must serve to function at a higher level. Why do employees often feel they are doing the nurse a favor by doing their job well and efficiently? Are they serving me or the patient? The patient, of course. Where does this reality get lost in the everyday functioning of the floor? Nurses, secretary, patient care assistant or the respiratory therapist, we all serve a role and all get paid an hourly salary to work a set number of hours. I'm "on the clock" but don't have anything that needs to be done.

Everyone has heard the expression "misery loves company." It really does hold true, and this is not always a bad thing. Let me give you a few examples. When you're discussing with a friend something about your spouse that just infuriates you, somehow it gives you comfort to hear that their spouse does the same thing. You hear that other people's children provide the same challenges. It is a crazy miserable day at work; everyone reading this has had more than one of them. What makes you angry? First, there is a nurse just hanging out in the nurses station gabbing. Second, the secretary is on her third break and you haven't taken one. Third, the patient care tech is nowhere to be found, and, of course, you have to tend to the person on the bedside commode.

We feel our anger rise up. This anger first stems from an altruistic source. You really, really, really did want to give great care to your patients that day, but were completely unable. Ultimately, your inability to accomplish this goal caused anger to well up in you. Now the question is who got the brunt of this frustration: the nurse, PCA, secretary, or patient? The more and more you steamed the less cordial and polite you were. Or did you actively try to solve the problem by indicating to your fellow co-worker that a little team work is needed here? Who is responsible for ensuring we function as a unit? Unresolved anger turns into resentment, which then turns into complacency, which turns into bad nursing, and at that point no one will ever function as a unit.

Picture another scenario. It is a crazy miserable day. You turn around to find all your co-workers in the same dilemma. The secretary is working as hard as she can to get the orders in, calling the doctors without prompting. The patient care assistant has been an angel and you're sure her wings will sprout any minute. Your fellow nurses are as slammed as you. Do you really think you will feel as frustrated and angry on that day? No, of course not. You all were in it together. We endured the same grievance; we chalked it up to the day and life of a nurse. Gave one for the Gipper, or something like that. We find ourselves cracking jokes in the kitchen as we choke down our lunch in order to keep functioning.

The hospitals want excellent patient care and guess what? We really want to give it. But the answer does not lie in more patient techs, more secretaries or even more nurses (all these things could help, but the underlying problems remains). There is obviously a fair patient/nurse ratio. But as we all know, one day you could have four patients and have the most miserable day and the next day have six and have the easiest day with adequate time to eat. So the answer lies in team work. To sum it up, we don't find ourselves as angry when we all have a bad day. So let's ensure that everyone has a good day. There is great pride in having done a job well, and so many nurses have felt it even though the reality of it is between them and God.

Once team work has been achieved, we begin systematically writing down all the processes that steal our time and don't produce better patient outcomes. The problem here is the person experiencing the problem doesn't have the time or energy to document anything. This is why facilities need to send people to the frontline to begin documenting daily problems and overbearing processes. Document each and every one of them. Insist that administration show studies on how this improves outcomes, because clinically because we can't see it. Then show them how 95% of the Nurses who actually take care of the patients don't agree, and of course document why you don't agree. So many of our complaints and issues are subjective. If subjective evidence is all you have to describe your argument, write it down. If Nurses across America report the same subjective evidence, it becomes objective evidence by the sheer volume of similar complaints.

How about a unit culture that believes and acts on the premise that it takes a community of health care professionals to accomplish the needs of all the patients? Let's just imagine if there was a philosophy of everyone has a good day and if the place is mayhem, we all have a bad day. Let's create a unit where everyone helps. Can secretaries and respiratory therapists get water or help turn a patient? Let's create policies that allow them to do just that. Hell, we create policies for everything else.

I've worked with phenomenal ancillary staff who gave excellent care, whether that care came in the form of taking off orders, administering a breathing treatment, or the most underrated service—"a bath". If health care institutions are feeling the crunch of doing more with less, then shouldn't that also mean we look beyond the Nurse when searching for cost cutting measures? When respiratory staff are not busy, could they help serve the unit versus sitting back in the respiratory room? I believe they should have to. I can't tell you how many times I just needed a boost, or someone to help me turn a patient, and there was no one available to help me. I have worked with so many wonderful, helpful, compassionate respiratory therapists who have helped me on numerous occasions turn and perform a complete linen change. When they help me, it is considered over and beyond the call of duty. Who defines "duty"? Is it our job description? Duty is defined by Webster as an obligation that must be performed for moral or legal reasons. [14]

In a stereotypical household, the woman takes care of the kids, does the laundry, cooks and does all the cleaning. I pointed out to my husband that I'm responsible for everything in this house (we had a lawn service at the time) and he "helps me". I also paid the bills and took care of home schooling our two children. The role of "helper" is far less stressful than the role of accountability. Not to mention the constant accolades, thank you so much,honey, for doing the dishes, thank you so much for cooking the meal. The role of helper requires gratitude to be handed out. Who thanks me when I perform all my duties? My husband did "help" a lot. When I pointed out this fact, he said, "you're right, I never thought of it like that." He said, "Let's start making some things my responsibility". We never got to that point because what we achieved was so far greater than designated roles. We became a team; we perceived the needs of the day and genuinely worked together to get the house clean, the kids fed, the homework done, the bible story read and everything else that occurred in a day. We achieved synergy on a regular basis.

Some weeks when his work was crazy, I took on the brunt of the responsibility, and when my efforts toward improving the world of Nursing kept me brainstorming at the computer, he took on the brunt of the responsibility. Our family became synergistic and our marriage took on a new level of mutual respect and love.

Nursing holds the bag every time. Until writing this book, I never really thought about the above reality. In the chain of successful patient care every link can break with minimal accountability leaving the very last link bearing the entire weight. Nursing is the last link left with the inevitable responsibility of caring for the patient, even at the failure of all other departments.

The Nurse is held to ultimate accountability while all those around her serve in the role of "helper" if they step out of their given roles. The patient care assistant didn't get the accu check; she was just too busy. The Nurse is responsible because the person needs to eat and may very well need insulin. The respiratory therapist working with you on a particular day doesn't have a high work ethic or was genuinely busy; the Nurse is responsible for suctioning the patient, changing out the cannula, replacing the soiled drain sponge, ordering clean new ties for around the trache. The Nurse is ultimately accountable, because the patient needs the secretions cleared to optimally breathe. The secretary takes off the orders and there is a list of supplies for a dressing change and an order that reads give Zyvox if okay with Dr. Kapoor. If she doesn't order the supplies or call Dr. Kapoor, the Nurse is ultimately responsible to ensure the above is carried out.

I asked a person from environmental if she could clean a bedside commode in the dirty utility, and she said no. "I'm too busy." She may very well have been, but who on a given unit sees the whole picture? I would have just done it myself, but my other sick patients also had needs, which, of course, I could barely meet. I had an eighty-year-old blind woman two days post back surgery who needed a large dose of lasix (water pill) and needed a bedside commode. It took me three hours to get the bedside commode, and when I did, no one was available to help her when she had to go. Keep in mind the Nursing assistant I worked with that day was excellent. Her name was Marie and she was genuinely trying to serve her designated rooms, but the needs were too great. When I asked other patient care assistants to help, they had no problem telling me that was not their assigned rooms. Great employees like Marie fall off the wagon of strong work ethics everyday. If she worked three days in a row, and every day she tried, but could never really meet the needs of her patients, she would finally give up. It is about teamwork, from all disciplines, from all departments.

I had a family member ask to have the tray warmed up while the dietician was in the room. The dietician felt no need to say, "Let me do that." It wasn't her job description. Someone from dietary came up to deliver a milk shake. I informed her that the person was moved to room 3619 and asked if she could take down a bag of clothes that was left in the room since she was going down to his room. She told me no, she didn't want to be responsible for someone's belongings. I called transport three times and asked if they could take the bag down. I meant to deliver the bag on my way out but forgot. I don't know if it ever got delivered.

So Nurses must always step out of their job description while the world around them has very defined boundaries. Nurses' job description: do everything concerning the patients' needs and make sure you hand out lots of accolades to everyone who helps you. Because you need help in whatever form you can get it,

When a Nurse works with people with high work ethics, the day is so much less stressful. We spend the day thanking people left and right because when someone is in the role of "helper," proper social etiquette mandates gratitude. And don't be mistaken, we are genuinely grateful! When I do my job well and take care of all the needs of my patients, who thanks me? Sometimes the patient, but generally speaking, no one. Lately I've been experiencing overt ingratitude from patients and families because they are frustrated with the system and I am the easiest target. The family members do not understand why their loved one had to wait to get turned and repositioned; I am the point of service and the object of their dissatisfaction.

This is not about Nurses being appreciated. This is about defining the environment while changing the commonly accepted roles of staff. The secretary, patient care assistant, environmental employee, dietician, dialysis nurse, IV team, or respiratory therapist are given roles of "helper" within the system if they ever step out of their job description or "duties." But yet the Nurse is expected to always step out of her role. We will run down to lab if the tube system is down, we will draw our own labs if phlebotomy can't get there, we will run down to dietary to get a tray if no one has time to deliver it, we will heat up a meal if it gets cold, we will clean the room after a discharge if another person needs the bed, we will enter orders if the secretary is just too busy. We used to do just about anything for the sake of our patients. Nurses across the country are saying we will **not,** we can't, we won't and because we as a population have stopped saying we will, the system is crumbling upon itself and administration is baffled. Unless the above gets dealt with, you will never solve this Nursing shortage.

Some respiratory therapists, nursing assistants, and secretaries feel Nurses get paid more, which should justify us having to work harder. Nurses are an invaluable asset to physicians. I'm sure there are Nurses who look at doctors and say the same thing. "You get paid the big bucks. It's not my job to cover your ass." No amount of money could make me want to become a doctor; they work such long hours (their quality time at home is limited at best) and they are on call every third night, on average. They, as a profession, are also experiencing the same oppression of governing bodies and of a health care system gone bad. So again, everyone must work together as a team if hospitals will survive.

CEO's and Nurses actually have a lot in common. We both run the institution, just from opposite ends of the spectrum. Every CEO out there is looking for someone to take something off her plate and every Nurse out there is looking for someone to take something off her plate. CEO's have a great deal of responsibilities; Nurses have people's lives at stake. Keep the question in the forefront of everyone's job: Whom do we all serve? You can't achieve synergy or team work if you can't *define and fix* the problems/pitfalls of the current system. Which means unless we have a huge value shift within hospitals across America, inpatient beds may very well become prime real estate sold off to the highest bidder.

The only problems people are motivated to fix are the ones that cause them discomfort. The person with the headache is the first to look for the Motrin. The hospital employees feeling the greatest pain these days are bedside Nurses. Listen for a moment about my analogy of a problem.

Everyone uses their side view mirrors for changing lanes or parking. Recall a moment when the mirror got pushed in (car wash/ someone hit it by accident). Whatever the case, the first time you go to use the side mirror, you're frustrated because you count on it to safely switch lanes and you can't see out of it. "I'll fix it when I get out." Sure enough you get back in the car and start driving again, forgetting to fix the mirror, but you think to yourself, "I'm fixing that mirror this time." How many times did you get in and out of the car until you finally remembered to fix that mirror? You could have forgotten four times to fix it. Each time the need became more acute, which set into place an action plan. "This time

I will fix it the minute I get out of the car." The point of the story is, you had to continually experience the problem and the effects of not having the use of that needed mirror before you did something about it.

If someone in the back seat told someone in the middle row about the problem, are they motivated to fix the problem? How again does that mirror affect me? Because from where I'm sitting I see just fine, I don't need that mirror to be a passenger. Nurses have been complaining for twenty plus years and administration has been saying, how again does that affect me? Fortunately and yet unfortunately, it does affect everyone and we need big picture thinkers who *feel* the problems. The pulse of any institution is at the bedside. I boldly state the profession of Nursing has a thready pulse at best (dying patient) and is getting ready to code.

I left the field for three years. Upon my return to inpatient care, in just under a week of service, the reality and frustrations of inpatient care came crashing in on me like a bad déjà vu. CEO's, CFO's, top nursing administrators have diligently searched for the magic septor that creates happy nurses and hence positive patient satisfaction surveys. What makes for happy nurses? Bonuses, higher pay, more staff? Yes, but yet no. The daily problems still exist, so being paid more doesn't provide the solution (although increasing Nurses' salaries is much needed). Do we as nurses seek to solve the daily frustration of our jobs? I have not really seen it.

Utopia in the day or night of a nurse: the medications are sitting there waiting for us to administer them, the nursing assistant did all the vitals and accu checks and documented them appropriately, all supplies were readily available and the secretary entered the orders promptly and ordered the necessary supplies listed on the order sheet without being prompted, and when the day does go crazy, your fellow nurses that aren't as busy come to your side to help.

Patients just want a little TLC

It is safe to say if a person is in the hospital, they are sick in some capacity, physically or mentally. This cannot be a person's best moment of the year. What makes patients happy? I have often felt the basic needs that Florence Nightingale and her followers started out providing have been lost by the masses of nurses. Nurses are brilliant and often much more knowledgeable on a given subject than the doctors they deal with. I have, through the years, learned many numbers and formulas and lab values and can honestly say I have given excellent patient care through my knowledge and advanced expertise in a field. The patient will never really know what we do for them through our excellent assessment skills and diligent follow through with the physicians. What they do remember are the little things.

So what is more important? I venture to say that a balance between the two must be obtained. I have many times found myself so behind because I couldn't help but tend to basic needs. Imagine not brushing your teeth for days. The person physically feels better after brushing his teeth. I'm telling you, it's an amazing phenomenon. Patients just want to be taken care of when they are sick. The fact that you are brilliant is a great thing, but this factor does not make the patient happier. We know it saves lives and better patient outcomes are achieved through the acts of brilliant nurses, but it doesn't give the patient a feeling of well being.

The kind word and the two minutes spent listening; the genuine effort to return with the coveted ice cubes for the patient that is not supposed to have anything by mouth. These things send patient satisfaction ratings off the chart. But when constantly triaging, the ice cubes keep getting pushed to the bottom of the list. We all have had that not-so-desirable patient to take care of. I have often used the expression "we all want to be loved". Now let's treat each person with respect. Let's start first with the classic alcoholic admitted for cirrhosis to cellulitis who is now experiencing withdrawal. This is the moment in a person's life they can rise above the situation to use super-human strength. Usually the person is filthy from a lack of personal interest or homelessness. Take the time to bathe this person. The feeling of worth and the good feeling that one feels when clean, prevails over the nastiness. I say try it. The belligerence decreases when one feels human. Clean sheets, a bath, and thirty minutes of your time will have a lasting impact. I promise you, your day will go easier and so will the patient's.

Never underestimate the spiritual impact of a bath; it transforms the person. The joy of being worthy of or just being clean in and of itself changed the person from the outside in. One, I looked at them differently. Two, they looked at themselves differently, and three, they were nicer for it. People know when they stink; they just don't care enough to do anything about it. How very sad.

Once I bathed a gentleman from head to toe with the help of an assistant. He grumbled, growled and cursed me out. His bed was soaked with urine from head to toe because he didn't care enough to use the urinal and didn't seem to care to lie in it either. Was I grossed out and disgusted by this? Of course I was. My disgust for this person should not prevail over my oath to take care of the human being; he did receive his bath. He actually received three baths because he kept urinating in his bed. During the third bath he was the most belligerent. I explained to him that it did not matter how many times he did this, I would bathe him again (the water got colder each time). "No patient of mine is going to lie in urine." He couldn't understand why I even cared, and at that moment his hardened heart relinquished. He got into the clean bed and slept like a baby, and yes, he also apologized for his ill behavior after his blissful nap in a clean bed. God blessed us both; by making the better choice to persevere, the rest of my day went better. If I hadn't made the better choice, he would have continued with his belligerence and I would have hardened my own heart. So we would have both been burdened with the sin of just not caring.

Everyone wants to be treated with respect, whether they have earned it or not. So very often the things that bring us into the hospital are years of bad living or stress. We must rise above ourselves everyday to serve the patients that we have promised to take care of. I listen to Christian music and pray the entire way to work and still have difficulty rising to the level of service that is needed. We are paid to serve our fellow man in their greatest time of need. Some people run out to the mission field, quit their jobs and sell all they have to do some noble cause. We get paid to do it, and if we choose to, we have the privilege of experiencing the same gratification of serving another human being.

People through the years that have been recognized for their awesome service to humanity. Martin Luther King, Mother Theresa, Gandhi, to name just a few. We as nurses are getting paid an hourly salary to serve our patients. Your heart may not be that of a servant, but you have contracted to provide a service for an hourly salary. Give the people what they are paying for. Twelve hours is a long time to work. I function at a high level right up to about 4 p.m., at which time I see a significant lack of oomph. Now imagine I'm a money hungry nurse working my fifth twelve hour shift in a row. Do you think I am rising above myself? I am merely functioning to the best of my abilities.

Chapter Eight

Mother Theresa as CEO

If a hundred people were asked if Mother Theresa was a great person and a powerful change agent? Most would say yes. What power did Mother Theresa have? By serving the poorest of the the poor through *acts* of kindness she accomplished miracles. By the worlds standards she had no actual power but yet yielded a world to see her vision and hope. The power lies in the act and ultimately in the action.

A visionary leader is one who is loved after their visions prove fruitful. Visionary leaders look at realities and then take a firm stand to change those realities that don't fit into their belief system. Martin Luther King believed in the future where mutual respect crossed racial barriers, it has happened. He remained among the people while solving the problems. Mother Teresa believed in a future where love would prevail to the poorest of the poor, she remained among the people while solving the problems. Nelson Mandela was loved and respected by his people, why you ask, because he also stayed connected, even from his jail cell.

Norman Borlaug was told his ideas about abolishing world hunger were "nutty" and yet he continued to astound people and continents, he received the Nobel Peace Prize, the Presidential Medal of Freedom and the Congressional Gold Medal[15]. This trifecta has only been achieved by Martin Luther King Jr., Mother Teresa, Nelson Mandela, and Elie Wiesel. Norman Borlaug believed in a world where hunger did not have to be a reality. In 1965 while he was working in Indo-Pakistan dodging artillery shells, he managed to increase agricultural output sevenfold. At the same time he was working on the problem of national hunger a book was published portraying doomsday in relation to food supplies. "The Population Bomb" made the national best seller list in 1968. One guy talking about the problem the other actively in the field trying to do something about the problem. Thousands of people writing about the Nursing shortage, but no one close enough to the problem to come up with any viable solutions to the problems at hand.

Elie Wiesel a holocaust survivor challenged and enlightened the world to rise above the state of indifference. The following quote is from a speech he gave in the East Room of the White House on April 12, 1999 as part of the Millennium Lecture series. "It is so much easier to look away from victims. It is so much easier to avoid such rude interruptions to our work, our dreams, our hopes. It is, after all, awkward, troublesome, to be involved in another person's pain and despair. Yet, for the person who is indifferent, his or her neighbors are of no consequence. And, therefore, their lives are meaningless."[16]

To survive as a Nurse within the inpatient setting you have to learn to look the other way. Being aware of and trying to tend to all the needs around you would be to physically and emotionally draining and after all everyone else has looked away. People walk through the unit all day long and close their eyes to the problems. The world of inpatient care has become a toxic environment to function within and those on the front line do their best just to survive while the world around them sits by idly.

If you live as a pacifist avoiding the problem is your only option, you have to remove yourself from the situation or ensure someone else is the target. Within the hospital setting someone has to be the target, someone has to take the difficult assignment, and everyone must avoid the really hard work to survive. Because on a good day, it is really just *A Good Day in Hell*. If you don't blend in well with the existing environment you set yourself up to become that target. History has proven, people will allow a group to be victimized just because they happen to be more vulnerable. Honor demands that someone try to protect them. I ask myself where are all the honorable people? I have seen and felt the pain of a very dysfunctional environment and everyone sits by idly. Year after year governing bodies give me one more task to accomplish and everyone sits by idly (the fact that it doesn't improve patient outcomes is irrelevant). I have felt and seen staff members brow beat another peer, everyone sits by idly. The employees who seem to survive the world of inpatient hospital care are the complete pacifist, the conformist, or the work around employee (avoiding the stress and the expense of others). Change agents are ostracized and weeded out. People are paralyzed in a state of inaction holding to the thought "I can't change it". Everyone working in a hospital serves the patient. Every day, every month, every year the job of all inpatient employees become more difficult and people are becoming increasingly indifferent to the needs around them.

The world listens to whom???? Every famous person mentioned above had dirt on their hands when they received those awards, none of them sat in lofty boardrooms, they broke mental barriers through adversity and suffering. They saw the problems first hand and shared in the suffering of others. Few are motivated to fix a problem for which they do not feel the resulting pain of. One of the many suggestions that I propose are that all registered Nurses should work on the floors a minimum of 2 days a months until this nursing shortage (which is quickly turning into a national crisis) is resolved. Change will only occur until people with actual power begin to feel the everyday frustration and yes "pain" of being a inpatient employee.

Hospitals now have a shortage of Nurses, as well as decreased revenue from insurance agencies. Profit or non-profit, no one likes to watch their net income go down each year. The big buzz is, do more with less. Hospitals across the country have allowed people and governing bodies who never touch a patient tell medical professionals how to implement care. People have not lost the joy of serving I boldly state the system has stolen that joy.

The process of becoming indifferent is a symptom of a bigger problem. Oppressive forces have enslaved inpatient staff, making it difficult for them to serve your loved one. The Nurse's work evaluation doesn't reflect how well she took care of your grandmother. Her evaluation reflects how well she *documented* the care of your grandmother. This process of indifference occurred through a system that scorned the lack of documentation more then it scorned the lack of care any given employee gives a patient. What has made working within the inpatient setting so burdensome? What or whom is oppressing the world of Nursing? Ultimately the system penalizes those Nurses who spend too much time with their patients. And everyone wonders why the environment within hospitals across the US has changed for the worse.

"True service is not something you do for God but something you let God do through you."

~Charles Stanley

"Leadership is not something you do to people, it's something you do with them."

~Ken Blanchard

The direct correlation between those two quotes hit home. So practicing good business techniques is just biblical. Who do we look up to for a vision and a hope? We do our jobs to the best of our abilities with the full knowledge that many of our efforts will go unseen. Our best efforts faint in comparison to Gods strength.

Upper level management work a minimal of sixty hours a week just to tread water and put out fires. Staying alive is the game, and in this game the treading executives are trying to reach a group that is doing just the same. Treading water trying to stay afloat mentally, physically, and spiritually, and we are now gasping for air. To continue to uphold a standard that can never be met is mentally exhausting. You must quit or lower the standard somewhere.

Tom Peters in his book *Thriving on Chaos* states;

> Ironically, the most lightly regarded people in most organizations, public or private, are those who are closest to the customer (patient, citizen) and most directly responsible for the quality and responsiveness of service delivered. This tradition must be reversed with a vengeance, if total customer responsiveness is to become reality.[17]

Nurses are not "lightly regarded" as much as they are misunderstood. Executive staff don't understand nurses; they smell different, their clothes look different. Let's starting asking our front line what the perceived problems are. Executive say to themselves, "I'll ask the nurse manager—she is a nurse after all. She wears a suit and is a little easier to talk to; she talks my language with a bit more fluency". News flash: she doesn't work as a nurse anymore. She now is in management and her stresses are not the stresses of a staff nurse. The nurse manager's object of service is now the CEO and the staff Nurses' object of service is the patient. Are we seeing the dichotomy here?

I do feel a priority shift needs to occur if any institution is going to increase Nurse satisfaction ratings and hence increase retention ratings. Happy Nurses don't complain. I often feel like I'm in a unique position when it comes to hierarchical lines of commands. I don't care who likes me; my job/goal is to give excellent patient care.

Let's keep the goal in the forefront of every organization. What is my goal for today? What is the most important aspect of my job? Finding a problem is easy; finding possible solutions is obviously more difficult. So whose job is it to find the solutions to the problems nurses present to administration? In the course of any given day, we usually work diligently, and people don't problem solve in the midst of chaos. When the pace slows, possible solutions are suggested. Now we are getting somewhere; Nurses are usually quite busy. Many Nurses find themselves barely taking thirty minutes during a thirteen-hour day.

So yes, we report problems, but we don't get paid to sit at round tables with lattes to discuss resolutions. Innovation—well, I guess that's something that happens at the top; those at the service line don't know what they really need. Better yet, let's pay a ton of money to some consultants that don't work as Nurses to tell us what we need. I know my behavior sounds a bit disrespectful, but my God, have I mentioned we have a soon to be national crisis on our hands? I'm not the "yes man" most organizations nurture. These are the problems, these are my solutions. If you have better solutions, let's hear them, let's do something. Nurses need to know administration cares enough to battle them out. Why do organizations even keep those yes men? Corporations pay these guys to take down the very ship they are suppose to be sailing and then everyone pats them on the back as the people are drowning.

Those who implement plans must make the plans. How basic but how rarely implemented. Give me the problems from the trenches and facilitate those involved to fix them. Who is most motivated to solve the problem? The person with it, of course! Whoever is actively trying to solve the problem has to remain within the environment so they can see and *feel* the problems.

Zig Ziglar states:

> "One person with a commitment can outperform 100 with an interest."

Those consultants regarding flows and process of an institution, (no medical knowledge), have an interest. Paying a Nurse to problem solve would still be cheaper and they would actually have some knowledge of the problem, unlike the consultant.

When the CEO/CFO/SVP is looking for structural/ financial / managerial solutions to problems, do they call someone from clinical positions (those who wear scrubs) to solve their problems? NO. They pay high powered consultants big bucks to tell them how to increase operating margins. They spend hundreds of thousands on financial, internal, and marketing consultants, and yet spend a six pence on the problems that exist with 33% of their operating costs. Yes, Nursing represents at least 33% of the operating cost of any given hospital. So why in God's green earth would you send someone in a suit (consultants/ upper administration) down to our world to solve our problems? The chasm is huge and if administration would begin acknowledging the differences, we can begin the process of bridge building between the two worlds. To try to create a team without first acknowledging inherent differences is showing disrespect.

How does this last sentence apply to the business of helping change the way inpatient units/hospitals function? How does this improve the job satisfaction of millions of Nurses and inpatient staff? Pilot projects, charters, team building and process changes are necessary but a waste of money if done by people too far removed from the realities they deal with. Generally, consultants are helpful advisors from a distance. People need to know you care. How do people show they care? They show they care by being present. Who is present for the Nurse? Cards and gifts are nice, as they let you know people are thinking of you (awards/memos/gift cards). Dinner delivered to your door is really nice, as it took time and effort (free luncheons). Having someone show up willing to do whatever needs to be done—laundry, dishes, deep cleaning, cooking, or the oh-so-undervalued act of active listening. Again the rhetorical question: who is present for the Nurse? For administration to tap into the heart of Nurses, someone needs to first just listen and then someone other than the Nurses needs to start getting their hands dirty. Spend a day with a Nurse. Physically try (which won't be easy) to help her with menial tasks. You may hold the title of Senior VP of seven campuses, but you can't even begin to do my job. Realizing this fact should invoke a sense of humility within the heart of everyone involved in hospitals at an executive level.

Peters asks the right questions in his book *Thriving on Chaos*:

What's the quality of direction being given to the workers?

Direction? you ask. The analogy here is you can go to the ball, Cinderella, after you get these insurmountable chores done. You can take care of your patients, dear staff, but not until you document that care and mark off all the boxes on some checklist. Oh yes, then you are allowed to take care of your patients.

Where's the opportunity for workers to contribute ideas about how to do the job better?

We have plenty of opportunity to contribute our innovative ideas, but when your ideas are continually disregarded, people stop investing precious energy. Administration cares more about what some regulating agency tells them versus what the flesh and bones that run the organization tell them about what works and what does not work. So we can theorize hospitals are enslaved themselves and haven't considered fighting the powers that be. Every hospital says, "Okay, what do you want me to do and how fast do you want me to do it?" when their accreditation is on the line. No one asks the unadulterated question of whether the recommendation actually provides better care. If it doesn't increase the quality of care I give my patients, take it off my plate.

Peters goes on to say further:

> "The real impediment to producing a higher-quality product more efficiently isn't the workers, union or nonunion; it's management."[18]

Well, can I get an AMEN from the congregation on that one. Somehow, someway people think if they ignore the problem long enough it will either go away or just be forgotten about. I really think when management finally gets a reprieve from complaints they think somehow all is well. If you haven't resolved the problem and you haven't heard how someone else has solved it. Why in God's green earth would you think it is no longer a problem? I feel like a kid who wants to scream from the top of her lungs, Duhhhh!

> "The day soldiers stop bringing you their problems is the day you stopped leading them. They have either lost confidence that you can help them or concluded that you do not care. Either case is a failure of leadership."[19]
>
> ~ General Colin Powell

The role of nurse manager

Now let's examine the role of the nurse manager. The reasons people choose to become nurse managers are varied, but let's assume for this discussion that there is a genuine desire to be a good leader. They now wear suits and are accepted by those business professionals we spoke of earlier. I suspect when they first entered into the business world, they felt like a fish out of water. Feeling a little intimidated by those in administration, they began their careers eager to please. Nurse manager RN (lets not forget our humble beginnings) holds a leadership role and they begin listening to the complaints/concerns of the staff—only to realize she doesn't know what to do with the same reoccurring problems that existed when she was a Nurse. When upper administration asks how are things going, the answer is "great." No one wants to admit they can't solve the problems on their units. So the wheel keeps turning.

The problems that exist are the same in all inpatient care settings just too varying degrees. This should give every nurse manager out there a sigh of relief. **No one** is documenting the problems that exist. But to document problems in their raw form may very well expose the bigger problem. No one has solved the problems of nurse dissatisfaction. If every nurse manager out there admitted to their superiors there is a real problem down here in the trenches, maybe the CEO/COO/SVP would begin asking the right questions. We would finally get the ball rolling, with some viable solutions.

I remember the surveys for employee satisfaction. The questions they asked did not even touch on what made my job difficult. One nurse said, "These questions were designed to make administration look good," and I could see why she would think that. But the reality is, no one would spend that kind of money in the middle of a health care crisis just to make themselves look good. But what it did tell me was that they truly and genuinely cared, but didn't have the slightest idea as to what the actual problems were.

We need a new approach to the problems that affect most of health care, and that is why I am writing this book. Surveys are useless unless people know action will result from their input. Take immediate action on surveys or at least investigate the results. I personally have not tangibly seen or felt the improvement of work conditions that resulted from a survey.

Where and when are inpatient unit staff allowed to meet on company time to resolve problems? Nurses cost the hospital a lot of money, and yes, you will have to spend more before you can begin to think of saving. In Peter's book *Thriving on Chaos* he tells how at Chaparral Steel, each operation has a problem-solving room, equipped exactly like the corporate boardroom. Could you picture twelve people in scrubs sitting in a decked-out boardroom? I think I like that idea.

Nurse managers don't tell their supervisors just how unhappy nurses really are. "My team is great. Numbers look good. They are doing meaningful work. The same usual insignificant problems but nothing serious." (You mean the same insignificant problems that are causing this national crisis). The complaints sound so childish. Well, we can't take on the oppressive governing bodies, so we find the outcomes we can change (schedule, assignments, admissions, discharges, role of charge nurse) and that is the *object* of our dissatisfaction but not the real catalyst to the problem at hand. What is the root cause of the dissatisfaction? You won't ever figure it out if you keep sending your employees from the office with "Play nice now, boys and girls."

What was the emotion fueling the squabble? For me, it was the inability to give the care I set out to give in the beginning of the day. For the other person, it may be the perceived lack of respect given to him or her from staff. Who knows? No one does, because the problems are never documented. One manager told me she had an employee who really believed he was purposefully given the patients with diarrhea. We all know how absurd that sounds; but we all know how calculated and cunning Nurses can be to those they don't like.

I overheard two Nurses doing just that, they were going to give the patient a laxative and then joked about how "that would be a good patient for Kevin." Come on, guys, we all know it happens. The least-liked Nurse gets the least-liked patients. Do you think I just started verbalizing my thoughts today? I once addressed an assistant nurse manager who worked night shift about my assignment (which made her mad). I can honestly say I got every chronic patient on that floor from that day forward. She taught me.

Actually she did, because that was the ultimate catalyst to this book and to the flood of problem-solving ideas. If I had gotten relief from the circumstances, my level of dissatisfaction may never have welled up to the point of NO MORE and I would have never pursued this endeavor. The job that followed allowed me the opportunity to float to every floor in the hospital, and then there was no stopping me. Floor after floor after floor, different people/patients/diagnoses and the same problems. I was one day verbalizing dissatisfaction with a checklist. My question was, does this improve the quality of care you give your patient? At that very moment a person from education walked in and the Nurse directed the question to her. My response was, "she doesn't take care of the patients. You do. I'm asking you." That Nurse would not answer the question, and at that point the charge Nurse said, "Kelly used to work with us but now she floats to all floors in the hospital to tell people her viewpoints." She smiled at me, and I just laughed inside. She was absolutely right. That was exactly what I was doing.

Maybe nurse mangers could give direct quotes from staff so they won't appear unprofessional. But the premise still holds true: people generally don't complain for the fun of it. Ninety-nine percent of the time there is an actual problem. Sometimes acknowledging the problem is half the battle. Not acknowledging actual or perceived problems halts the resolution process. This is the place hospitals are at right now. Give me the problems from the trenches and help them facilitate the resolution process. Let's tap into that wellspring of anger and frustration. The fact you hear complaints says they still care enough to say something about it.

I just love this quote. Let's read it again:

> "The day soldiers stop bringing you their problems is the day you stopped leading them. They have either lost confidence that you can help them or concluded that you do not care. Either case is a failure of leadership."[20]
>
> ~ General Colin Powell

Respect is gained by acknowledging what you don't know. Respect is gained when you give an extra thirty minutes a day to work on a problem that you don't perceive is yours. So very often nurse managers think these moments of dissatisfaction will just pass and they do, with no real resolution having been found.

Business tends to function in lines of promotions, important projects, roles of leadership, and, of course, new and important titles. Nursing career track are quite lateral. So the nurse who has remained a staff nurse for forty years still holds the job title of staff Nurse. We must give ourselves promotions. Which is partly why nurses like to stay in a given field. Nurses become ostentatious, admiring our own abilities and knowledge base while putting down our peers for service that pales in comparison to our own. I know pathophysiology better than anyone else. I can decipher lab values better than anyone else. My mastery in cardiology is unmatched by many doctors. I understand and can teach the subject of disseminated intravascular coagulation (trust me this is a tricky one). Although no one gives us titles, we earn respect in a given area. We should start acknowledging our individualized promotions. Heck, we could start handing out promotions to each other, acknowledging the strength in each Nurse. The premise on raising nurses is to tell them what they are doing wrong. Let's start telling what we admire in each other.

Chapter Nine

The Path from Me to WE

S peaking out is hard. You ultimately place your-self in a position to be talked about. Does anyone really want to be talked about? Not really. Because the harsh reality is people like to talk trash. When people talk, they don't say, "Oh, that Curnayn girl. Isn't she amazing? Look how she is breaking down barriers." No, the conversation is more like, "Who the hell does she think she is? When does she have time to think of all these things? Maybe she should work more; she'd have less time to stir the pot." Most people who speak out have a certain amount of genuine courage. Speaking out does not have to equal troublemaker.

Here are the differentiating qualities between trouble maker and innovator:

Trouble Makers
    a. Love to hear themselves talk.
    b. Talk loudly about frustrations.

   c. Rarely have viable solutions.

   d. Don't like to professionally argue opposing viewpoints. "This just stinks."

   e. Tries and often effectively takes down morale.

Is that courage somewhat displaced by the troublemaker? Somewhat. Address the troublemakers' concerns. Usually there is some validity to the statements. This can often be difficult because giving a troublemaker the reins often results in a stampede. Your best bet is to cut this person off at the pass when publicly speaking; it's better to speak with the troublemaker one-on-one. They feel validated while not sabotaging the efforts of the meeting. Status quo people don't accomplish anything, so let's embrace passion whatever form it comes in.

Innovators

   a. Love to listen to others *after* their opinion and thoughts are heard.

   b. They speak out above the crowd when verbalizing opinions and ideas and are usually quite impassioned. But the true difference here is they will intently listen to the answers given because they genuinely want the problem fixed.

   c. Innovators come to the table with plausible ideas on how to approach solving the problems.

   d. Love to hear and professionally battle out opposing viewpoints. "I could change my view on the subject if the person could prove his reasoning."

e. They are outspoken employees with a sincere intent to change the system. They try to present the problems without destroying the morale of other employees. I never bad-mouthed the institution—just discussed the problems that existed within the system. For me, the system represents every unit, floor, hospital in the entire US. I'm not picking favorites.

So how can someone continually bring up problems without sounding negative? Let's just say it is difficult. Because I am obviously emotionally tied to the problems, emotion had to drive me to a passion that resulted in a mission to change the system. The key difference for me was, I went through the process of typing out my frustrations on Microsoft Word. The emotion behind a problem is the first step in problem resolution. So when it was time to find out from others what their frustrations were, I could remain calm but yet empathetic. I developmentally had moved from frustration to searching for solutions, and problem-solving is an entirely different emotion than helpless frustration with no perceived solution in sight.

In my case, the problems that existed were so blaring, yet no one discussed them. Nurses weren't happy and administration's worst fear was getting the troops riled up. I believe they sincerely thought keeping them at bay would suffice. Here I would come, Kellyann, constantly asking all the dreaded questions. I have to say if you get a Nurse talking about the problems that exist within the field, you had better have the time to listen.

So why does no one (staff and administration) really delve into the cause of these problems?

Some theories of mine:

1. Ignorance is bliss. Why have someone pour her heart and soul out when you don't feel you have any resources (physical or mental) to help her resolve the issues that are communicated? Dealing with a problem appropriately creates buy-in toward the organization, even if the resolutions are not immediate. An incident/problem not dealt with leads to apathy.

2. People aren't reporting the problems and those that do, don't have enough buy-in to care about being part of the solution. Which is why my services are so desperately needed. At first I will be the inexhaustible listener for every employee on any given unit. Once the cat's out of the bag, then everyone's problems are laid out on the table. How empowering it will be for staff to see someone acknowledging their problems as real. Many of the inherent problems in the system will take years to fix, but staff will at least see the glimmer of hope which comes in the form of action, someone with a pair of scrubs willing to do any job you throw at her.

3. Change is miserably hard at first. If we have an impending national crisis and a constant shortage of Nurses, administration wants peace above all. You must stay focused on the goal; the intent of the heart is to give excellent patient care while also improving job satisfaction. True change requires a certain level of anarchy. Think about training children; was it not anarchy when you expected a higher level of functioning, but after achieving the new milestone, didn't the child develop a greater sense of self? No I'm not making a comparison to raising children, I'm making a comparison to the difficulty of making lasting changes in the hearts of human beings. Apathy is a difficult state to move passed which makes the problems within the world of inpatient care all the more ominous to take on.

4. Institutions *manage* people to the lowest common denominator instead of raising the bar to the self-motivated, excellent employee. I say again, the person hanging around the corner would have a greater level of job and personal satisfaction if someone held her to a higher level of service. The person with a higher level of service is continually discouraged by the lack of accountability held to those *team* members that fall below the bar. My daughter is probably the most responsible child you will ever meet and takes offense when someone treats her below the level

of maturity and trust that she has already achieved at the age of nine. When not given the respect she deserves and earned, her work ethic and performance go down accordingly.

5. Our enemy has remained elusive and no one wants to take on Goliath. Who is Goliath accountable to?

"The chief reason for our failure in world-class competition is our failure to tap our work force's potential."[21]

~ *Tom Peters*

Everyone involved in the inpatient setting sees the problem from her own viewpoint. Think about all the money spent on retention and recruitment, only to send newly recruited Nurses into a dysfunctional environment. Retention efforts are hard to see from a bedside perspective. As far as I can see, hospital organizations no longer have a choice. Nurses are a huge financial stake in the financing of American health care.

The bigger question is why don't Nurses want to get involved? Well, hospital organizations, Nurses have been verbalizing dissatisfaction for over twenty years. Why should we get involved? "My job drains the life blood out of me nearly every day I punch in. Do you really think I'm going to invest another minute on that unit?" "You want me to invest my 'off' time to help resolve problems that you as administration don't acknowledge as real?" So what you really are saying is please come in paid or unpaid and improve the things that administration wants done. Now, I understand. You want me to implement resolutions that someone from upper administration has mandated, because they know what the problems are. Every hospital would love to receive Magnet status, oooohhh, ahhhhh, the gold star for any hospital CEO. You need the buy in from Nurses to make the above a passing thought. And it is no big secret, you can't get buy in if you can't get them involved.

Writing this book was difficult because I lost the privilege of punching out. I did not physically work as a Nurse many hours while writing this, but my mind had to be constantly engaged in the perceived and actual problems of nursing. I had to constantly place myself mentally in the mucky water. The problems that exist in nursing remind me of the family secret that everyone knows about but no one speaks of. Nurses don't go home after a thirteen-hour day and sit at our computers and start writing about it. We come home, unwind, and gear up for another day. If we've had too many days off, many nurses felt anxious, depressed, or just moody the day before they returned to work. No one likes to hear themselves moan, groan, and complain, so we pull up our boot straps and take it like a woman. But the problems still exist and hence we punch in and punch out to maintain our sanity.

Unveiling the Problems

1. Start asking new graduates for their honest opinion, without the influence of administra-

tion. The interviewer cannot be someone who could repeat these statements to staff. Being accepted and respected as a new graduate is crucial to survival.

2. Ask new employees for recommendations. Every environment has its own dysfunctional behavior. The new employee will not have yet become engrained in the behaviors of the new environment.

3. If you ever get a Nurse who hasn't worked for a few years and returns to the field for whatever reason, soak up every word she has to say. She is not a graduate nurse right out of school—just a little rusty. When an experienced good Nurse returns to the field, she comes in with great deal more confidence and wisdom.

4. Listen to your staff and document all reported problems. Often the problems seem small. Example: My assignment is unfair. View every problem as the result of a bigger one, because generally speaking, it is. Maybe that person's assignment is not fair; maybe every assignment on that unit is not fair based on fair labor laws. But if the person doesn't **see** everyone else experiencing the same problem they feel unjustly treated. START DOCUMENTING.

5. Start, just start, doing something, because the gift certificates are not going to retain your Nurses over the long haul.

Actual and Perceived Problems

1. Too many variable stresses in the course of a day. This one ultimately encompasses the reasons for Nurse job dissatisfaction and the dysfunction that ensues from such stress. Now to dissect each one of those stresses and begin changing the system is the real job.

2. Nursing holds the bag every time. Orders written, unrealistic policies to implement, lab work that needs to be done, vitals that need to be taken, orders that need to be entered, and, of course, the usual duties that encompass the day and the life of a nurse. The weight of this bag is taking us under.

3. The day is really just too long but the time off is just great. Hard balance here. Eight hours are easier to work, hands down, but I don't see that happening.

4. I don't think Nurses are overly concerned with our image, that whole "handmaiden" theory articles refer to. We demand respect and we get it, I don't see a real problem here. Now how we demand is not always in the most functional ways, but whatever the case, we get respect.

5. Nurses strike out at each other because they are stressed out on all sides with no hope of reprieve.

Solutions (just some)

1. Have every hospital employee spend at least one day with a Nurse. Let them see how their job affects that front line

2. Ask those in educational and administrative roles to step back into clinical roles for two days a month.

3. Spend money on looking at the actual problems within the field of Nursing. Hospitals are expanding and building to be ready for the expected needs of the community while they spend a fraction on solving the problems within Nursing. Halt construction, guys. There are no Nurses to staff those new buildings.

4. Teamwork, all committed to the greater cause. Empowered employees would be able to move mountains.

5. Rotate charge nurses. This is a role used as a respite for weary nurses and they can also use this role to take care of their buds. I know this idea won't buy me popularity with those that now function as charge nurses, and not every charge nurse out there abuses the role. This book is written to improve the quality of life for every nurse, not just a select few. My very first job we rotated the role of charge. Some people were better than others within this role, but we all were well aware of what it took to make the floor function in the course of a day. We functioned more as a team. Much of the

role of charge nurse involves coordinating activities with med management and helping with any crisis that may arise.

Becoming a Nurse is not an easy task. Our curriculum consisted of chemistry, micro-biology, anatomy and physiology, and then nursing school. So it is safe to say we as a group of people are above average in intelligence. But yet only a handful are qualified to function as charge Nurse. Performing the role of charge Nurse is something every employee of one year or more could do.

6. Nurses round as facilitators so an average med surg unit with forty beds must have at least sixty nurses. Each nurse remains in the role for a week. He or she facilitates problem resolution; all problems are filtered through her first. Keep a log/journal of on-going problems. Document all problems and list reasons for inability to resolve at this time. If the problem is documented a thousand times in one year, administration needs to validate that it is real. As of now, all we hear is murmuring.

Why remain so structured all the time? Allow the facilitator to problem solve on the fly. Let him or her live among the insanity. When someone is upset and frustrated, ask the questions: What would make your life easier right now? What can I do for you right now? When we start documenting the "right now," then we will begin to unveil the problems of everyday life on a Nursing unit.

7. Systematically remove or improve every process, machine, and code that steals the health care provider's time and doesn't increase the quality of care we give our patients.

Changing a system requires passion—a genuine desire for the outcomes. Passion can't be bottled or paid for. Passion is just that—a desire that goes far beyond the paycheck but a drive that no amount of opposition can swelter. Corporations are intimidated and put off by those who have too much passion. Frankly, I think people realize they don't have that spark and are afraid that person might take their job. You're right, they will, so the lesson here is get impassioned about something. Find a job that doesn't have people as your product.

When consultants are brought in to study flows and processes on a unit, their point of service is executive staff. If executives are happy, their companies look good. What makes executives happy and what makes bedside care providers happy are worlds apart. My vision for Me to We Consulting is to serve the inpatient staff and ultimately the patients they serve. How can anyone implement effective change with a population of people, if those people are not the object of your service? No one has defined the "why" behind the shortage or the growing dissatisfaction within the inpatient world. This company's approach is unique, in a world where everyone is looking for the lofty positions of supposed great influence. To lead, you must stay connected. Me to We Inc. (MTW) was created under the premise of connectedness.

One of my objectives is to create an environment that people will want to work in not because of how administration treats us but because of how we (inpatient staff) treat each other. The day-to-day grind is what determines *overall* retention rates (not the health or retirement plan).

Someone must administer the elixir that reverses the process of cardiac damage before myopathy sets its. Let's document unnecessary and useless processes and present the facts to the bigger giants. Bring in a consulting team of nurses, patient care assistants and secretaries to function as staff and listen to those working on the floors. Hear the complaints of every staff member working on the unit and actually do something with the complaints. Work with each and every employee on the unit to come up with viable solutions. Then feverishly document the trends across the U.S. and use those numbers to force change across the country. Allow the employees to take an active role while helping them facilitate their plan. Help create an environment so they can get a breath of fresh air. When you are constantly in the muck struggling to get air, there is not a lot of problem solving taking place. Secretaries will respect another secretary who can do their job and a patient care assistant will respect and confide in someone who understands her unique complaints. Nurses will respect the position of another Nurse, side-by-side doing patient care, not too good to take on any job, while still displaying an excellent knowledge base of pathophysiology and critical care. Only when you gain the respect of bedside staff will you be able to make lasting changes. Everyone wants to get out of working on the floors but they have no problem telling their subordinates what should be done. Don't tell me you know why my job is so difficult until you have done it.

"Ultimately we are never really happy until we experience the joy of serving others."
Kellyann Curnayn

The Need for Workers
Matthew 9: 35-38

[35]Jesus went through all the towns and villages, teaching in their synagogues, preaching the good news of the kingdom and healing every disease and sickness. When he saw the crowds, he had compassion on them, because they were harassed and helpless, like sheep without a shepherd. Then he said to his disciples, "The harvest is so plentiful, but the workers are few. [38]Ask the Lord of the harvest, therefore, to send out workers into his harvest field."

Bibliography

Alter, Jonathan, (2007), *He only saved a Billion People* http://www.msnbc.msn.com/id/19886675/site/newsweek/page/0, *(July 2007)*.

Blanchard, Ken & Muchnick, Mac (2003) *The Leadership Pill; The Missing Ingredient in Motivating People Today*: Free Press

Blanchard, Ken & Bowles, Sheldon (2007). *High Five* (Compact Disc). Harper Collins Publishers Inc

Chambers, Oswald. (1992) *My Utmost for his Highest: Special Updated Edition*. Oswald Chambers Publications Association, Ltd.

Herbelin, Steve (2000). *Work Team Coaching*. CA: Riverbank Books

Hiam, Alex (2002). *Making Horses Drink: How to Lead and succeed in business*. Entrepreneur Media, Inc.

In Touch. ®magazine Aug 2006, vol. 29 No.8. Copyright 2006

Katselas, Milton (1996). *Dreams into Action*. Dove Books

Peters, Tom. Thriving on Chaos. 1987 Alfred A Knoff, Inc.

The Holy Bible (1984). New International Version. Zondervan Bible Publishers.

Stanley, Charles Dr. (4 Compact CD's) Servanthood: The Way to Greatness. In Touch Ministries.

Zig Ziglar. Goals: Setting and Achieving them on Schedule. (audio cassettes) Simon & Schuster.

Endnotes

1 Charles Stanley, "Satisfaction through Servanthood," *In Touch* (August 2006), p.7.

2 James Carville and Paul Begala, *Buck up Suck up and Come Back When You Foul Up,* (Simon and Schuster NY, 2002), p.197.

3 Ann Landers, *Sarasota Herald-Tribune*, (October 11, 1998).

4 Charles Stanley, "Satisfaction through Servanthood," *In Touch* (August 2006), p.7.

5 Charles Stanley, "Satisfaction Through Servanthood," *In Touch* (August 2006).

6 Oswald Chambers, *My Utmost for his Highest: Special Edition* (Oswald Chambers Publication Association, Ltd., 1992). February 23 daily devotional>

[7] Milton Katselas, *Dreams in Action,* (Dove Books, 1996), p. 39>

[8] Bernard Shaw, *Maxims for the Revolutionists,* http://www.bartleby.com/157/6.html (May 2007).

[9] Alex Hiam, *Making Horses Drink* (Entrepreneur Media Inc, 2002), p. 201

[10] *What is Behind HRSA's Projected Supply, Demand and Shortage of Registered Nurses?* ftp://ftp.hrsa.gov/bhpr/workforce/behindshortage.pdf, (Nov 2006).

[11] *Hospital Medication Errors may be on the Rise,* (Dec 2003), http://findarticles.com/p/articles/mi_m0815/is_12_28/ai_110843029, (Feb 2007).

[12] James Carville and Paul Begala, *Buck Up Suck Up and Come Back When You Foul Up* (Simon and Schuster NY, 2002), p. 173.

[13] Oswald Chambers, *My Utmost for his Highest: Special Edition* (Oswald Chambers Publication Association, Ltd., 1992). January 9th daily devotional.

[14] *Webster's Universal English Dictionary,* (Geddes & Grosset, 2005), p.96.

[15] Jonathan Alter, *He Only save a Billion People,* http://www.msnbc.msn.com/id/19886675/site/newsweek/page/0/, (July 2007).

[16] Elie Wisel, *Elie Wiesel,* http://www.winnersx.com/world/wiesel-winnerx.htm (July 2007).

[17] Tom Peters, *Thriving on Chaos,* (Alfred A Knoff, Inc., 1987), p.172.

[18] Tom Peters, *Thriving on Chaos,* (Alfred A Knoff, Inc., 1987), p.412.

[19] Alex Hiam, *Making Horses Drink,* Entrepreneur Media Inc., 2002), p. 117.

[20] Alex Hiam, *Making Horses Drink,* Entrepreneur Media Inc., 2002), p. 117.

[21] Tom Peters, *Thriving on Chaos,* (Alfred A Knoff, Inc., 1987), p. 286.

Me to We Consulting

PO BOX 954136
Lake Mary, FL
32795-4136

Business   407-323-2333
Toll Free   866-521-2333
Fax   407-330-3555

MetoWeConsulting.com

Printed in the United States
92583LV00001B/1-99/A

9 781604 771725